David Filo

The Yahoo Co-Creator's Real Story – Unofficial

Mohammed Okafor

ISBN: 9781779699374
Imprint: The More You Read The Bigger It Gets

Contents

Introduction

The life and legacy of David Filo

Who is David Filo?

David Filo is a legendary figure in the world of technology, best known for being the co-founder of Yahoo, one of the most iconic internet brands of all time. Born on April 20, 1966, in Wisconsin, David Filo had a humble upbringing that laid the foundation for his future success.

Growing up in Wisconsin, David was intrigued by technology from a young age. He was fascinated by computers and spent countless hours tinkering with them, eager to understand how they worked. This early exposure to technology sparked his passion for computer science, a field that would later define his career.

As David's knowledge and love for computers grew, so did his ambition. He envisioned a way to organize and categorize the vast amount of information available on the internet, which was still in its infancy at the time. This brilliant idea laid the groundwork for what would eventually become Yahoo.

After graduating from high school, David left his small-town life behind and headed to Stanford University to pursue a degree in computer science. It was during his time at Stanford that he would meet his future business partner, Jerry Yang, and together they would embark on an incredible journey that would revolutionize the internet.

At Stanford, David and Jerry joined forces on a project to create a curated web directory called "Jerry and David's Guide to the World Wide Web," which was essentially the prototype for Yahoo. This project, initially started as a hobby, soon gained momentum and became a sensation among users.

The breakthrough moment for David and Jerry came when they realized the enormous potential of their creation. They recognized that the internet was rapidly expanding and there was a need for a comprehensive search engine to navigate and make sense of the growing amount of online information. This realization led to the decision to drop out of Stanford and fully dedicate themselves to developing Yahoo.

With their innovative directory-based approach, David and Jerry were able to offer users a simple and intuitive way to discover websites, greatly improving the web browsing experience. The name "Yahoo" was chosen because it represented the enthusiasm and exclamation people often make when they find something exciting.

Yahoo quickly gained popularity and attracted millions of users. It became a go-to destination for people searching for information, news, email services, and much more. The rapid growth and success of Yahoo transformed it into one of the most influential companies in the history of the internet.

David Filo's role in shaping Yahoo's success cannot be overstated. He was the technical wizard behind Yahoo's infrastructure and played a crucial role in scaling the platform to handle the ever-increasing traffic. His genius as a programmer and his dedication to creating a user-friendly experience were instrumental in Yahoo's rise to dominance.

Despite facing challenges and fierce competition from the likes of Google, David Filo remained committed to Yahoo's mission of organizing the world's information and making it universally accessible. Through strategic acquisitions and partnerships, he ensured that Yahoo stayed relevant and continued to evolve with the changing landscape of the internet.

While David Filo's journey is undoubtedly filled with triumphs, it hasn't been without its fair share of setbacks. The dot-com bubble of the early 2000s posed a significant threat to Yahoo's survival, but David's resilience and strategic decision-making helped the company weather the storm and emerge as a global internet powerhouse.

Beyond his role at Yahoo, David Filo has remained actively involved in the tech industry. He has invested in numerous startups and continues to support and nurture young entrepreneurs. Moreover, he is known for his philanthropic endeavors, using his wealth to make a positive impact on society.

David Filo's legacy extends far beyond the confines of Yahoo. His contributions to the tech industry have inspired countless programmers and entrepreneurs to push the boundaries of what is possible. His determination, innovative thinking, and unwavering commitment to the user experience are lessons that aspiring technologists can learn from.

As we delve deeper into the life and career of David Filo, we will uncover the challenges he faced, the triumphs he celebrated, and the invaluable wisdom he gained along the way. Through his journey, we will gain insights into the evolution of the internet, the power of a groundbreaking idea, and the path to success in the ever-changing world of technology. So, buckle up and prepare to be inspired by the story of David Filo, the visionary co-creator of Yahoo.

The birth of Yahoo

In order to understand the birth of Yahoo, we need to go back to the early days of the internet, a time of immense possibilities and untapped potential. It was during this time that two young computer enthusiasts, David Filo and Jerry Yang, embarked on a journey that would change the internet landscape forever.

1.1.2.1 The internet revolution The internet revolution of the 1990s brought about a new era of information sharing and connectivity. People from around the world were now able to connect, communicate, and share knowledge in ways that were previously unimaginable.

1.1.2.2 The emergence of web directories As the internet grew rapidly, the need arose for tools that could help users navigate through the vast amount of information available. This is where web directories stepped in. These online platforms served as organized collections of websites, offering users a way to search and discover relevant content.

1.1.2.3 David Filo's vision David Filo, a computer science graduate student at Stanford University, recognized the need for a better web directory. With his keen understanding of technology and a passion for organizing information, Filo set out to create a platform that would revolutionize web search and browsing.

1.1.2.4 The early development stages In the early 1990s, Filo started cataloging his favorite websites and organizing them into a hierarchical structure. He called it "Jerry and David's Guide to the World Wide Web," named after himself and his friend Jerry Yang. This guide served as the foundation for what would later become Yahoo.

1.1.2.5 Collaborative efforts with Jerry Yang David Filo's serendipitous encounter with Jerry Yang, also a Stanford student, proved to be a turning point in the history of Yahoo. Yang shared Filo's passion for organizing the web, and the two decided to combine their efforts to create a more comprehensive and user-friendly web directory.

1.1.2.6 The creation of Yahoo In January 1994, Filo and Yang transformed their web directory project into a website named "Yahoo!" The name, an acronym for "Yet Another Hierarchical Officious Oracle," reflected the playful spirit of the early internet era.

1.1.2.7 The power of Yahoo's directory What set Yahoo apart from other web directories of the time was its meticulous organization and intuitive user interface.

Filo and Yang manually categorized the websites and diligently curated the content, allowing users to easily navigate through the vast online landscape.

1.1.2.8 Yahoo's early success Yahoo quickly gained popularity among internet users who were hungry for a reliable and user-friendly web directory. The platform's attention to detail, comprehensive coverage, and engaging user experience propelled it to the forefront of the emerging internet industry.

1.1.2.9 The seed of innovation Yahoo's success as a web directory laid the foundation for further innovation. As internet usage and technology continued to evolve, Filo and Yang seized opportunities to expand Yahoo's services beyond just a directory, transforming it into a full-fledged internet portal.

1.1.2.10 Yahoo's impact on the internet landscape Yahoo's birth marked the beginning of a new chapter in the internet's history. It not only revolutionized web browsing and search but also paved the way for other internet giants to rise. Yahoo's influence can still be felt today, as it played a critical role in shaping the internet as we know it.

1.1.2.11 Lessons from Yahoo's birth The birth of Yahoo teaches us the importance of recognizing the needs and opportunities presented by a rapidly changing technological landscape. It highlights the power of collaboration, meticulous organization, and a commitment to providing users with the best possible experience.

In the next section, we will delve into the early years and education of David Filo, exploring the influences that shaped his journey towards co-creating Yahoo.

The impact of Yahoo on the internet

Yahoo's impact on the internet cannot be overstated. In its early years, Yahoo was a pioneer in organizing and categorizing the chaotic world of the internet, providing a sense of structure and order to a rapidly expanding digital frontier. The web directory created by David Filo and Jerry Yang revolutionized the way people searched for information online, laying the foundation for the modern search engines we use today.

1. The organization of information: Yahoo's web directory was a breakthrough concept in the late 1990s. It allowed users to navigate the vastness of the internet by categorizing websites into various topics. This organization made it easier for users to find relevant information, providing a sense of direction in the otherwise uncharted waters of the World Wide Web. Yahoo's curated approach to indexing websites brought a human touch to the search experience, distinguishing it from the algorithm-driven search engines that would later dominate the market.

Example: Imagine being a student researching a term paper on marine biology. Before Yahoo, you would have had to wade through countless unrelated websites to find the information you needed. However, with Yahoo's web directory, you could simply navigate to the "Science" category and find a subcategory specifically dedicated to marine biology, drastically reducing the time and effort required to find credible sources.

2. Expansion of user base: Yahoo played a significant role in expanding the internet's user base. By making the internet more accessible and user-friendly, Yahoo attracted millions of users who were previously intimidated by the complexity of the online world.

Example: Consider a middle-aged individual who had little exposure to computers and the internet. The simplicity and organization provided by Yahoo made it easier for them to dip their toes into the digital realm. By offering a user-friendly interface, Yahoo helped bridge the gap between the online and offline worlds, allowing a wider audience to engage with the internet.

3. Diversification of online services: Yahoo not only focused on search, but it also diversified its services to cater to a broader range of user needs. From email and news to finance and entertainment, Yahoo became a one-stop destination for internet users, offering a platform where they could access a variety of services without needing numerous accounts.

Example: Imagine a busy professional who wants to catch up on the latest news, communicate with colleagues via email, and manage their finances all in one place. Yahoo provided a seamless experience by integrating news articles, email services, and financial tools into its platform, eliminating the need for the user to switch between multiple websites and applications.

4. Setting the stage for online advertising: Yahoo's success in attracting a vast user base made it an attractive platform for advertisers. It pioneered the monetization of the internet through display advertising, allowing businesses to promote their products and services to a global audience.

Example: Consider a small business looking to reach a wider market. Yahoo's advertising platform offered targeted advertising options, allowing businesses to reach specific demographics or user interests. This level of granularity enabled businesses to maximize their advertising budget and improve their return on investment.

Overall, Yahoo's impact on the internet was profound. It transformed the way people accessed and interacted with online information, making it more organized, accessible, and user-friendly. Yahoo's legacy lies not only in its pioneering efforts but also in its role as a catalyst for the growth and globalization of the internet. By laying the groundwork for future search engines and online services, Yahoo set the stage for the digital revolution that continues to shape our world today.

Key Takeaways:

- Yahoo's web directory brought structure and organization to the early internet, revolutionizing the way people searched for information online.
- Yahoo expanded the internet's user base by making it more accessible and user-friendly.
- Yahoo's diversified services made it a one-stop destination for various user needs, eliminating the need for multiple accounts.
- Yahoo's success in attracting users paved the way for online advertising, enabling businesses to reach a global audience.

Further Reading:

- Levy, S. (2010). In the Plex: How Google Thinks, Works, and Shapes Our Lives. Simon & Schuster.
- Vise, D. A., & Malseed, M. (2006). The Google Story. Random House.
- Miller, M. (2011). Yahoo! The Ultimate Guide to the Web 2001. Pengrove Press.

By exploring Yahoo's impact on the internet, we gain a deeper understanding of the forces that shaped the digital landscape and continue to influence how we navigate and interact with online information. In the next section, we will delve into the reasons behind writing an unofficial biography of David Filo and explore his journey from a young programmer to a co-creator of one of the most influential companies in internet history.

Why write an unofficial biography?

Writing an unofficial biography about David Filo is an opportunity to delve into the fascinating story of a man who played a crucial role in shaping the internet as we know it today. It allows us to explore the untold aspects of his journey, shedding light on the challenges, triumphs, and personal experiences that influenced his path.

Unofficial biographies provide a unique perspective, free from bias or restrictions often found in official accounts. They offer the freedom to capture the real essence of a person, highlighting their successes, failures, and everything in between. Through this lens, we can understand the motivations, decisions, and struggles that influenced David Filo's life and career.

By writing an unofficial biography, we can delve into the untold stories and shed light on the lesser-known aspects of David Filo's journey. Official biographies often focus on the highlights and achievements while leaving out the more humanizing details that make an individual relatable. By exploring the lesser-known moments and personal anecdotes, we can paint a more complete picture of David Filo as a person, not just a famous programmer.

An unofficial biography allows us to capture the essence of David Filo's character, his inspirations, and challenges in a way that connects with readers on a more personal level. It is an opportunity to present the man behind the co-creation of Yahoo, showcasing his struggles, perseverance, and the lessons he learned along the way.

Furthermore, an unofficial biography provides the freedom to draw connections to broader themes and trends in the tech industry. We can explore the impact of Yahoo on the internet, the challenges it faced in the face of competition, and its eventual decline. It allows us to reflect on the lessons learned from the Yahoo experience and how they shaped the future of technology and the internet.

Writing an unofficial biography also allows us to celebrate the legacy of David Filo, not just as a co-creator of Yahoo but as a significant contributor to the tech industry. We can highlight his impact, both in terms of technological innovation and business strategies, and how his work continues to inspire future programmers and entrepreneurs.

This unofficial biography is an invitation to readers to join in the exploration of David Filo's life, legacy, and the enduring influence of Yahoo. It is an opportunity to reflect on the lessons learned, appreciate the challenges faced, and gain insights from a remarkable journey that continues to shape our digital world.

Tricky Trivia: Did you know that Yahoo was originally named "Jerry and David's Guide to the World Wide Web"? The name "Yahoo" was adopted later as an acronym for "Yet Another Hierarchical Officious Oracle." It was chosen partly because it was short and memorable, making it more accessible to users.

Early Years and Education

Growing up in Wisconsin

The influence of technology on young David

David Filo grew up in a small town in Wisconsin, surrounded by the beautiful countryside and the serenity of nature. However, it was not just the natural landscape that captured his attention, but also the world of technology that was gradually unfolding around him.

A curious mind and early exposure to technology

From a young age, David had a curious mind and a natural inclination towards understanding how things worked. He was always tinkering with gadgets and exploring the inner workings of his toys. It was clear to anyone who knew him that he had an innate curiosity and a passion for problem-solving.

Technology was not readily available in David's early years, especially in a small town like his. However, David's insatiable curiosity led him to seek out opportunities to explore the world of technology. He would spend hours reading books, magazines, and any other resources he could get his hands on to satisfy his thirst for knowledge.

A transformative encounter with computers

It was during David's teenage years that he had a transformative encounter with computers. The local library in his town received a donation of a few outdated computers, and David was immediately drawn to them. These computers, although not cutting-edge by any means, were a gateway to a world of possibilities for young David.

David spent countless hours at the library, devouring books on computer science and programming. He taught himself the basic concepts of coding and began experimenting with writing simple programs. This newfound passion for computers consumed him and became a driving force in his life.

The spark of inspiration

As David's knowledge and skills in computer science grew, he started to envision the potential of technology to transform the world. He saw computers not just as a tool for personal use but as a means to connect people, disseminate information, and bridge the gaps between different communities.

This revolutionary idea became the spark that ignited David's imagination. He began to dream of creating a platform that would bring people together, enable them to share knowledge, and ultimately make the world a smaller and more interconnected place.

The birth of Yahoo in David's mind

While attending high school, David Filo's mind was constantly abuzz with ideas of how to use technology to build something that would change the world. It was during his formative years that the concept of Yahoo gradually took shape in his mind.

Inspired by his love for the internet and his passion for organizing information, David envisioned a web directory that would provide users with a comprehensive and organized list of websites. The idea was to make it easier for people to navigate the vast expanse of the internet and find relevant information quickly.

The road to Stanford University

Determined to pursue his dreams, David set his sights on Stanford University, a renowned institution known for its prestigious computer science program. Leaving behind his small town in Wisconsin, he embarked on a new chapter in his life.

At Stanford, David found himself surrounded by like-minded individuals who shared his passion for technology. The stimulating environment and the countless opportunities to learn and collaborate further fueled his ambition to create something meaningful and impactful.

The importance of a supportive community

David Filo's achievements were not solely a result of his individual brilliance but were also deeply influenced by the supportive community he found at Stanford. The camaraderie among students, the mentorship from professors, and the collaborative nature of the computer science department created an environment that nurtured innovation and encouraged bold ideas.

It was within this community that David met Jerry Yang, a kindred spirit who shared his vision and became his partner in creating Yahoo. Their collaboration and complementary skills were instrumental in turning David's vision into a reality.

Lessons learned from David Filo's journey

David Filo's journey serves as an inspiration to aspiring programmers around the world. It underscores the importance of curiosity, persistence, and an unwavering belief in the transformative power of technology.

From his humble beginnings in a small town to co-creating one of the most iconic internet companies in history, David Filo's story is a testament to the impact one person can make through their passion and vision.

The enduring influence of Yahoo's success

Yahoo's success not only made David Filo a household name but also left an indelible mark on the internet as we know it. Through Yahoo, David and his team pioneered many of the features and technologies that are now staples of the online experience.

From search engines to web directories, from email services to news aggregators, Yahoo laid the groundwork for much of what we take for granted in the digital age. This enduring influence is a testament to David's foresight and the impact he had on shaping the direction of the internet.

Looking towards the future

As we reflect on David Filo's journey and the influence of technology on his life, it is crucial to consider the future. The world of technology continues to evolve rapidly, presenting new challenges and opportunities.

For aspiring programmers and tech enthusiasts, David Filo's story is a reminder that innovation knows no boundaries. It is a call to push the limits of what is possible and to strive for solutions that can transform the lives of millions.

In the next section, we will delve deeper into David Filo's early years at Stanford University and his encounter with Jerry Yang, which set the stage for the birth of Yahoo. Stay tuned as we uncover the fascinating story of how two individuals changed the internet forever.

A passion for computer science

David Filo's journey in computer science began during his formative years in Wisconsin. Growing up in a small town, he was introduced to the world of technology at a young age.

The influence of technology on young David

In a time when personal computers were still a novelty, David's curiosity was piqued by the machines he encountered. From early on, he showed an innate understanding of technology and an eagerness to explore its potential. Whether it was tinkering with radios or building basic electronic circuits, David's passion for understanding how things worked was evident.

A pivotal moment: discovering computer science

David's true calling came when he got his hands on his first computer. It was an eye-opening experience that ignited his fascination with coding and problem-solving. He spent countless hours experimenting with programming languages, teaching himself the fundamentals of computer science.

A self-driven journey: the birth of Yahoo in David's mind

While still in high school, David began envisioning the possibilities of using computers to connect people and share information. The idea of a comprehensive web directory, where users could easily find and access websites, started to take shape in his mind. This vision would eventually become the foundation of Yahoo.

Leaving Wisconsin for Stanford University

Determined to further his education and pursue his passion, David left his hometown and headed to Stanford University. The prestigious institution provided him with the perfect platform to broaden his knowledge and delve deeper into the world of computer science.

Embracing the challenges of computer science

At Stanford, David encountered a vibrant community of like-minded individuals who shared his passion for technology. The rigorous curriculum pushed his problem-solving skills to new heights, fostering his love for the field. He actively participated in coding competitions, where he honed his programming abilities and showcased his potential as a top-notch coder.

Inspiring mentors: meeting Jerry Yang

During his time at Stanford, David also had the opportunity to meet Jerry Yang, who would later become his co-founder at Yahoo. Their shared passion for computer science and their complementary skills formed the foundation of a lifelong partnership.

Unconventional learning: the development of Yahoo as a hobby

While still immersed in his studies, David and Jerry began developing Yahoo as a hobby project. Little did they know that this endeavor would soon turn into a worldwide phenomenon. The duo constantly pushed the boundaries of what was possible, combining their deep technical knowledge with their creative ideas to shape the future of the internet.

Embracing the entrepreneurial spirit: dropping out of Stanford

As Yahoo started to gain traction, David and Jerry faced a critical decision. With the immense potential of their creation becoming apparent, they made the bold choice to drop out of Stanford and dedicate themselves fully to building Yahoo into a successful company. This pivotal moment would define their careers and shape the course of internet history.

The unwavering passion

Throughout David Filo's journey in computer science, one thing remained constant: his unwavering passion for the field. His insatiable hunger for knowledge, his ability to think outside the box, and his love for innovative problem-solving set him apart. David Filo's deep-rooted passion for computer science would continue to shape his life and the world of technology for years to come.

The next section will delve into the birth of Yahoo and the incredible impact it had on the internet. Stay tuned for an adventurous ride through the early days of Yahoo's growth and the challenges it faced along the way.

The birth of Yahoo in David's mind

The story of Yahoo begins with a young and ambitious David Filo, whose passion for computer science was ignited during his early years in Wisconsin. Growing up in a world increasingly driven by technology, David found solace in the possibilities that computers offered. His fascination with this emerging field planted the seed for what would later become one of the most influential companies in internet history.

The influence of technology on young David's life cannot be overstated. From an early age, he was captivated by the power of computers and their ability to transform the world. Whether it was tinkering with his first computer or programming simple games, David's interest in computer science continued to grow.

It was during his high school years that David's entrepreneurial spirit began to take shape. He noticed the rising popularity of the internet and saw the potential it held for connecting people and sharing information. The idea of creating a platform that could organize and categorize the vast amount of online content was something that excited him.

As David's passion for computer science deepened, so did his vision for a web directory that could revolutionize the way people found information online. He saw the internet as a chaotic space in need of structure and organization. Inspired by his experiences, David started brainstorming ways to bring order to the digital realm.

During his time at Stanford University, David's path intersected with that of Jerry Yang, another brilliant mind in the world of computer science. This meeting would prove to be the catalyst for the birth of Yahoo. David and Jerry quickly bonded over their shared passion for the internet and their belief in its potential to reshape the world.

As their friendship grew, David and Jerry began discussing their ideas for a web directory that could simplify the process of finding information online. Together, they envisioned a platform that would provide users with a curated list of websites, classified into various categories and subcategories.

The breakthrough moment came when David and Jerry realized that their web directory could be automated using a hierarchical structure. This structure would allow for the efficient organization and categorization of websites, making it easier for users to navigate the vast online landscape.

With this realization, David and Jerry knew they had stumbled upon something groundbreaking. They decided to dedicate their time and energy to developing this idea further, believing that their web directory had the potential to change the way people interacted with the internet.

Dropping out of Stanford was a risky decision, but David and Jerry were fueled by their passion and determination. They saw the opportunity to bring their vision to life and felt that staying in school would only delay their progress. With their minds set on building their web directory, they made the bold choice to leave Stanford behind.

And so, the birth of Yahoo began with two young visionaries who were willing to take risks and pursue their dreams. Little did they know that their creation would go on to become one of the most iconic brands in the history of the internet.

As we delve deeper into the story of David Filo and Yahoo, we will uncover the challenges they faced, the triumphs they celebrated, and the lasting impact they have had on the world of technology. But first, let us explore the early years and education that shaped David's extraordinary journey.

Leaving Wisconsin for Stanford University

Leaving behind the serene landscapes of Wisconsin, David Filo embarked on a journey that would change his life forever. His insatiable curiosity and passion for computer science led him to Stanford University, where he would soon meet his future co-founder, Jerry Yang. But before we dive into that fateful meeting, let's explore the early years that shaped David's path to Stanford.

2.1 Growing up in Wisconsin

David Filo grew up in a small town in Wisconsin, surrounded by the natural beauty of the countryside. His childhood was marked by exploration and a deep fascination with technology. Even at a young age, David was enchanted by the merging of science and machines, which would eventually become his driving force.

2.1.1 The influence of technology on young David

As a child, David was exposed to the wonders of technology through his father, who worked as an electrical and electronics engineer. The sight of his father's workshop, filled with circuit boards, wires, and gadgets, ignited a spark within David. He spent countless hours tinkering and experimenting with various electronic components, learning the inner workings of these devices.

2.1.2 A passion for computer science

David's enthusiasm for technology took on a new dimension when he discovered computer science. In high school, he became engrossed in programming and software development. The logical thinking and problem-solving nature of coding became his obsession, leading him to seek out every opportunity to expand his knowledge in this rapidly evolving field.

2.1.3 The birth of Yahoo in David's mind

It was during his high school years that the idea of Yahoo began taking shape in David's mind. He envisioned a tool that would allow people to navigate the vast and chaotic world of the emerging internet. This vision would soon evolve into the groundbreaking web directory that would drive Yahoo's early success.

2.1.4 Leaving Wisconsin for Stanford University

Driven by his determination to pursue his passion for computer science, David took the bold step of leaving his familiar surroundings in Wisconsin and heading to Stanford University. Stanford's prestigious Computer Science program was renowned for cultivating some of the brightest minds in the technology industry.

The transition from a small town to a bustling campus was an eye-opening experience for David. The energy and enthusiasm of the academic environment fueled his desire to learn and create. Surrounded by like-minded individuals, he found inspiration, mentorship, and opportunities that would shape his future.

At Stanford, David immersed himself in a myriad of computer science courses, exposing himself to cutting-edge technologies, programming languages, and computational theories. These foundational principles laid the groundwork for his future endeavors and instilled in him a deep understanding of the inner workings of computers and networks.

2.2 Stanford years

2.2.1 Meeting Jerry Yang

While studying at Stanford, David had a serendipitous encounter that would alter the course of his life. He crossed paths with another ambitious student named Jerry Yang, who shared his passion for technology. United by their common interests, the two formed a bond that would prove instrumental in the creation of Yahoo.

2.2.2 The development of Yahoo as a hobby

With their complementary skills and shared vision, David and Jerry began experimenting with directory-style websites as a hobby. They painstakingly curated and organized lists of their favorite websites, identifying patterns and categorizing them for easy navigation. This labor of love was the embryo of what would later become the Yahoo web directory.

2.2.3 The breakthrough moment

David and Jerry's hobby project took a significant leap forward when they realized the potential for their web directory to solve a crucial problem: the chaos of the early internet. Their breakthrough came when they discovered a way to automate the process of compiling and updating the directory, making it more efficient and user-friendly.

This innovative approach attracted the attention of their peers and Stanford faculty members, who marveled at the duo's ability to harness the power of technology to organize the seemingly infinite expanse of the internet. The positive feedback motivated David and Jerry to take their project to the next level.

2.2.4 Dropping out of Stanford

The success and growing popularity of their web directory presented David and Jerry with a life-altering decision. Faced with the opportunity to turn their passion project into a full-fledged business, they made the bold choice to drop out of Stanford and dedicate themselves entirely to Yahoo's development.

By leaving behind the traditional academic path, David and Jerry embraced the uncertainty and risk inherent in entrepreneurship. They trusted their instincts and believed in the potential impact of their creation. Little did they know that their decision to leave Stanford would set them on a remarkable journey that would forever reshape the internet landscape.

In the next section, we will delve into the birth of Yahoo and the early days of its operations, as David and Jerry transform their hobby project into a global internet powerhouse.

Unconventional trick: When leaving their comfort zones, David and Jerry had no idea how radically their lives would change. Sometimes, taking a leap of faith can lead to unexpected opportunities and immense personal growth. The key is to follow your passion and believe in your vision, even in uncertain circumstances. Just like David and Jerry, dare to step outside of your comfort zone and embrace the unknown. It may be the very thing that propels you towards success.

Stanford years

Meeting Jerry Yang

Meeting Jerry Yang was a pivotal moment in David Filo's life. It was during their time at Stanford University that the two would form a bond that would lead to the creation of one of the most influential companies in the history of the internet. This section explores their initial encounter, the development of their friendship, and the eventual partnership that launched Yahoo.

A Chance Encounter

Jerry Yang and David Filo first crossed paths during their early years at Stanford University. Both pursuing degrees in electrical engineering, they shared a passion for computers and technology that would soon bring them together. Their initial meeting was serendipitous, occurring in one of their shared computer science classes.

David was immediately struck by Jerry's intelligence and technical prowess. He recognized Jerry as someone who could match his own skills and ambition, and the two quickly became friends. They bonded over late-night coding sessions, exchanging ideas and pushing each other to explore new frontiers in computer science.

Shared Vision and Common Goals

While David Filo harbored aspirations of creating a comprehensive indexed catalog of the emerging internet, he found a kindred spirit in Jerry Yang. They both saw the potential of the World Wide Web as a tool for organizing information and connecting people. This shared vision became the foundation for their partnership.

Jerry's entrepreneurial spirit and business acumen complemented David's technical expertise. They shared a common goal of organizing the chaotic web and making it more accessible to the average user. They believed that the internet could be a powerful tool for not just academics and researchers but for everyone seeking information and entertainment.

Building a Web Directory

As the web continued to grow at an unprecedented pace, David and Jerry realized the need for a centralized directory that categorized and indexed websites. They harnessed their combined skills to create a rudimentary web directory that eventually became the precursor to Yahoo.

Their directory was initially a hobby project, a way for the two friends to organize their growing list of favorite websites. They manually curated the listings, organizing them into categories and subcategories. Each new day brought new discoveries, and the directory expanded rapidly.

The Birth of Yahoo

One day, while brainstorming a name for their project, David jokingly suggested the acronym "Yet Another Hierarchical Officious Oracle" (YAHOO). And just like that, Yahoo had a name that would become synonymous with the internet.

With the directory gaining popularity among their friends and colleagues, David and Jerry realized they had stumbled upon something significant. They decided to take a leap of faith and expand their hobby into a fully-fledged business. They dropped out of Stanford University to focus all their attention on Yahoo, believing they were onto something that could change the digital landscape forever.

The Power of Collaboration

David Filo and Jerry Yang's partnership exemplified the power of collaboration. They combined their complementary skills, technical know-how, and vision to create a platform that transformed the way people accessed and interacted with information online. Their ability to work together and leverage each other's strengths played a crucial role in Yahoo's success.

Their story serves as a reminder that partnerships and teamwork are often the key to achieving extraordinary results. In the fast-paced world of technology, collaboration can lead to innovative breakthroughs that revolutionize entire industries.

Unconventional Problem Solving

One example of David and Jerry's unconventional problem-solving approach was their decision to create a web directory manually. In an era before sophisticated algorithms and web crawlers, they curated Yahoo's listings by hand, categorizing websites based on their content.

While this approach was time-consuming and required tremendous effort, it allowed them to develop a deep understanding of the web and its intricacies. It also ensured that Yahoo's listings were accurate and useful, providing users with a curated selection of high-quality websites.

This unconventional approach not only set Yahoo apart from its competitors but also laid the groundwork for the company's future success. It highlighted the importance of attention to detail, thoroughness, and a human touch in the rapidly evolving digital landscape.

Conclusion

Meeting Jerry Yang proved to be a turning point in David Filo's life. Their friendship and partnership would lead to the creation of Yahoo, forever changing the way people navigate and search the internet. Their shared vision, collaboration, and unconventional problem-solving set them apart from their peers and laid the foundation for Yahoo's enduring legacy.

In the next section, we will explore the development of Yahoo as a hobby and its eventual transition into a dominant internet brand.

The development of Yahoo as a hobby

In this section, we delve into the fascinating story of how Yahoo developed from a hobby into one of the most influential companies on the internet. It all began during David Filo's time at Stanford University, where he met his future business partner, Jerry Yang.

Meeting Jerry Yang

David Filo and Jerry Yang were both studying at Stanford University in the early 1990s, pursuing degrees in Electrical Engineering. It was during this time that Filo and Yang became friends and discovered their shared passion for technology and the emerging field of computer science.

Filo and Yang quickly realized they had a mutual interest in organizing and categorizing information on the internet, which was still in its infancy. They saw the vast potential of the World Wide Web but felt overwhelmed by the lack of organization and structure in the available websites.

The development of an idea

Fueled by their curiosity and desire to make the internet more user-friendly, Filo and Yang began developing a web directory as a personal project. They initially created a list of their favorite websites, organizing them into various categories based on topics.

As they continued to add more websites to their directory, they realized the need for a more systematic approach. They implemented a hierarchical structure, where websites were grouped into subcategories, making it easier for users to navigate the directory.

Building the foundation

What started as a side project soon consumed Filo and Yang's free time. They spent countless hours adding new websites to their directory, carefully evaluating each one for relevance and quality. This dedication and attention to detail set Yahoo apart from other directories that were either automated or lacked human curation.

Filo and Yang developed a reputation for their meticulous approach, personally visiting websites to determine their inclusion in the Yahoo directory. They believed that human judgment was essential in providing users with a reliable and comprehensive web resource.

The breakthrough moment

During the development of Yahoo, Filo and Yang faced a significant challenge – the sheer volume of websites being created and added to the internet. As the number of websites grew exponentially, it became impossible for Filo and Yang to maintain the directory manually.

To overcome this challenge, they developed a web crawler, a program that automatically scanned the web for new websites and added them to the Yahoo directory. This innovative solution allowed Yahoo to keep pace with the rapid growth of the internet and expanded its reach beyond what Filo and Yang could achieve manually.

From hobby to Stanford University's homepage

As the popularity of Yahoo grew, it started gaining attention beyond Filo and Yang's immediate circle. In 1994, Stanford University recognized the value of Yahoo as a resource and made it the default homepage for its network users.

This endorsement from a prestigious institution like Stanford further bolstered Yahoo's credibility and increased its user base. It also provided Filo and Yang with the validation and support they needed to take their hobby to the next level.

Dropping out of Stanford

With the success and growing demands of Yahoo, Filo and Yang made the difficult decision to drop out of Stanford University to fully dedicate themselves to their creation. They realized that Yahoo had the potential to revolutionize the way people accessed and organized information on the internet.

Leaving their formal education behind, Filo and Yang embarked on a remarkable journey, transforming their hobby into a groundbreaking internet company. The decision to drop out of Stanford was a pivotal moment in both their lives, paving the way for Yahoo's rapid growth and establishment as an influential player in the tech industry.

Conclusion

The development of Yahoo as a hobby from Filo and Yang's shared passion for organizing and categorizing information on the internet is a testament to their foresight and commitment. Their dedication to creating a reliable and user-friendly web resource laid the foundation for Yahoo's future success.

In the next section, we will explore the birth of Yahoo itself as Filo and Yang take their hobby to new heights and navigate the challenges and triumphs of building a global internet powerhouse.

Dropping out of Stanford

After a few years at Stanford University, David Filo found himself at a crossroads. His passion for computer science burned brightly, and he was eager to pursue his dream of creating a revolutionary technology. It was during this time that the seeds of Yahoo began to take root in David's mind.

2.2.4.1 The struggle of balancing academics and innovation

As David delved deeper into his computer science studies at Stanford, he began to realize that the rigid academic structure of the university was stifling his creativity. The traditional curriculum focused on theory and research, leaving little room for practical application and innovation. David yearned for a space where he could explore his ideas freely, unbound by the constraints of the classroom.

2.2.4.2 Fanning the flames of entrepreneurial spirit

Fueled by his desire to create something groundbreaking, David decided to take a leap of faith and drop out of Stanford. This decision was not taken lightly, as David understood the potential consequences of leaving behind a prestigious university education. However, he believed that his true education would come from the real-world experience of building a startup, rather than from the confines of a classroom.

2.2.4.3 The birth of Yahoo as a full-time endeavor

With his newfound freedom, David threw himself into the development of Yahoo. What had started as a hobby and web directory rapidly became a full-time endeavor. Alongside his friend and fellow Stanford student Jerry Yang, David worked tirelessly to expand and refine Yahoo's services. They recognized the power and potential of the internet and were determined to harness it in a way that would change the landscape of the digital world.

2.2.4.4 Embracing risk and defying expectations

Dropping out of Stanford was a risk, but for David Filo, it was a risk worth taking. He believed in his vision and was willing to defy societal expectations in order to pursue his dreams. This act of courage and conviction would shape the course of his life, forever solidifying him as one of the pioneering figures in the tech industry.

2.2.4.5 The unconventional path to success

David Filo's decision to drop out of Stanford may seem unconventional, but it is a testament to the unpredictable nature of success. In a world that often champions traditional educational paths, David's story serves as a reminder that sometimes the greatest growth and innovation come from stepping outside the confines of the expected. It is a lesson in taking risks, embracing failure, and forging ahead on one's own terms.

2.2.4.6 The value of real-world experience

While Stanford provided a strong foundation in computer science, David Filo recognized the value of real-world experience. By immersing himself in the world of startups and entrepreneurship, he gained invaluable insights, skills, and connections that would prove instrumental in Yahoo's success. This unconventional approach to education showcases the importance of hands-on learning and the power of the entrepreneurial spirit.

2.2.4.7 Inspiring future entrepreneurs

David Filo's decision to drop out of Stanford serves as an inspiration for aspiring entrepreneurs. It challenges the notion that success can only be achieved through traditional educational paths and encourages individuals to follow their passions and embrace the unconventional. David's story reminds us that the road to success is rarely linear, and sometimes, the greatest achievements come from taking risks and charting our own paths.

In the next section, we will explore the birth of Yahoo and the initial challenges David Filo and Jerry Yang faced in bringing their vision to life. We will delve into the creation of Yahoo's web directory and the crucial decisions that propelled the company forward. Through their determination and ingenuity, David and Jerry revolutionized the internet and established Yahoo as a dominant force in the digital world.

The Birth of Yahoo

The initial idea

The creation of a web directory

In the early days of the internet, the sheer amount of information available was overwhelming. There was no efficient way to navigate through the vast expanse of websites and webpages. David Filo recognized this problem and saw an opportunity to create a solution that would revolutionize the internet. This is the story of how he and Jerry Yang came up with the idea of creating a web directory called Yahoo.

The information overload on the internet

At the time when David Filo and Jerry Yang were brainstorming ideas for their project, the internet was rapidly expanding. Websites were being created at an unprecedented rate, and users were struggling to find relevant information amidst the digital chaos. The need for a comprehensive and organized directory of websites became increasingly apparent.

The vision of a web directory

David and Jerry imagined a platform that would act as a centralized hub, categorizing websites into specific topics and making it easier for users to find what they were looking for. Their vision was to create a curated list of websites, manually organized by a team of experts who would review and categorize each entry.

The manual curation process

The creation of Yahoo's web directory involved an extensive manual curation process. David Filo and Jerry Yang, along with a team of dedicated individuals, scoured the internet to find websites that were relevant and informative. Each website was carefully reviewed and categorized based on its content.

To ensure the accuracy and quality of the directory, the team had to establish a set of guidelines for categorization. This involved defining clear criteria for each category and subcategory, as well as developing a consistent approach to organizing websites.

The challenges of scalability

As the internet continued to expand, the manual curation process became increasingly challenging. The number of websites was growing exponentially, and maintaining an up-to-date and comprehensive directory required significant effort and resources.

To address this challenge, David Filo and Jerry Yang had to come up with innovative solutions. They introduced automation technologies to help streamline the categorization process. This allowed them to scale their operations and accommodate the growing number of websites.

The evolving nature of the web directory

While initially focused on organizing websites into categories, Yahoo's web directory evolved over time. David Filo and Jerry Yang realized that users needed more than just a listing of websites; they needed a platform that could provide relevant and personalized search results.

To meet this demand, Yahoo incorporated search functionality into its web directory. This enabled users to search for specific keywords or phrases and find websites that matched their search criteria. The integration of search technology marked a significant milestone in Yahoo's evolution and set the stage for its future success.

An unconventional approach

David Filo and Jerry Yang's approach to creating a web directory was unconventional in many ways. Unlike other search engines of the time, Yahoo prioritized human curation over algorithmic indexing. This allowed them to create a more curated and organized directory, providing users with a more reliable and accurate source of information.

Additionally, Yahoo's focus on user experience and personalized search results set it apart from its competitors. By combining manual curation with user-friendly search functionality, Yahoo was able to offer a unique and valuable service to its users.

Real-world applications

The creation of Yahoo's web directory had a profound impact on the internet landscape. It offered users a reliable and efficient way to navigate through the vast amount of information on the web. This not only revolutionized the way people accessed information but also paved the way for the development of future search engines and online directories.

Moreover, the concept of manual curation and human expertise in organizing digital content remains relevant in today's world. Many websites and platforms still rely on the expertise of curators and editors to ensure the quality and accuracy of information.

Further Exploration:

To learn more about the early days of Yahoo and the challenges of creating a web directory, I recommend reading "Becoming Yahoo: How David Filo and Jerry Yang Transformed the Internet" by David Bank. This book provides a firsthand account of the journey of Yahoo's co-founders and offers valuable insights into the birth of the web directory.

For a deeper understanding of the impact of web directories and search engines on the internet, "The Search: How Google and Its Rivals Rewrote the Rules of Business and Transformed Our Culture" by John Battelle is an excellent resource. It explores the history and significance of search engines in shaping the digital landscape.

Finally, for readers interested in the future of web directories and online search, "The Filter Bubble: What the Internet Is Hiding from You" by Eli Pariser offers a critical perspective on the personalized nature of search results and its implications for the dissemination of information.

Exercises:

1. Think about the challenges David Filo and Jerry Yang faced in manually curating the Yahoo web directory. How would you address these challenges in today's digital landscape? Discuss the advantages and disadvantages of human curation compared to algorithmic indexing.

2. Research and compare the early web directories to the modern search engines. How has the evolution of search technology impacted the way we access and consume information? Provide examples to support your analysis.

3. Imagine you are tasked with creating a web directory for a specific niche or industry. Develop a plan for how you would curate and organize the websites within

your directory. Consider the criteria for categorization and the challenges you might encounter.

The name "Yahoo"

One of the most intriguing aspects of the Yahoo story is the origin of its name. The name "Yahoo" has become synonymous with the internet giant, but how did David Filo and Jerry Yang come up with such a unique and memorable name?

The story behind the name "Yahoo" is a fascinating one and provides insight into the creativity and humor of the founders. It all started during a brainstorming session in the early days of Yahoo's development.

Filo and Yang were searching for a catchy and distinctive name that would capture the essence of their web directory. They wanted a name that would convey a sense of excitement, energy, and enthusiasm. They were looking for a word that was easy to remember and pronounce, yet carried a certain whimsical charm.

During this brainstorming session, the founders went through a long list of possible names. Many ideas were thrown around, but none seemed to capture the spirit they were looking for. It was then that Filo stumbled upon the word "yahoo" in Jonathan Swift's novel, "Gulliver's Travels."

In the novel, "yahoo" is used to describe a race of primitive and uncivilized beings. They are depicted as being irrational, impulsive, and prone to wild behavior. Filo found this word amusing and believed it captured the unpredictable and dynamic nature of the internet.

In a moment of inspiration, Filo suggested the name "Yahoo" to Yang, and they both immediately knew it was the perfect fit for their web directory. It was unconventional, catchy, and had a certain playfulness that resonated with their vision for the company. The founders also liked the fact that "Yahoo" was a unique and distinct word that was unlikely to be confused with any other brand.

Choosing the name "Yahoo" was a bold move. At the time, most internet companies had more formal and serious names. But Filo and Yang were not afraid to break the mold and take a risk. They believed that the name would capture people's attention and leave a lasting impression.

Little did they know just how influential and iconic the name "Yahoo" would become. It would go on to define a generation of internet users and become a household name around the world.

The name "Yahoo" perfectly encapsulates the spirit of the company and its mission. It represents the adventure and excitement of exploring the vast universe of information on the internet. It embodies the unconventional and daring approach that Filo and Yang took in revolutionizing the way we navigate and interact with the online world.

In conclusion, the name "Yahoo" is more than just a random assortment of letters. It is a symbol of innovation, creativity, and the indomitable spirit of its founders. It is a name that continues to inspire and captivate, reminding us of the incredible journey of David Filo, Jerry Yang, and their groundbreaking creation.

The early days of Yahoo's operations

The early days of Yahoo were filled with excitement, challenges, and a relentless pursuit of creating something revolutionary. David Filo and Jerry Yang, the co-creators of Yahoo, embarked on this journey with a simple web directory and a vision to organize the chaos of the internet.

The creation of a web directory

In the mid-1990s, the internet was rapidly expanding, with millions of websites popping up every day. However, there was a growing problem - finding relevant and reliable information was becoming increasingly difficult. This is where the idea of a web directory came into play.

David Filo, with his keen eye for organization and categorization, started compiling a list of interesting websites and organizing them into various topics. He manually curated the directory, putting websites into categories and subcategories based on their content. This was no small feat considering the sheer volume of websites on the internet at the time.

The goal was to create a comprehensive index of the internet, making it easier for users to find what they were looking for. It was a noble mission, but one that required constant effort and attention to keep up with the rapidly evolving web.

The name "Yahoo"

As David Filo and Jerry Yang continued to refine and expand their web directory, they needed a name that would capture the spirit of their endeavor. After brainstorming and tossing around various ideas, they settled on the name "Yahoo."

The term "Yahoo" originated from Jonathan Swift's novel "Gulliver's Travels," in which it referred to a race of beings that were grotesque and uncivilized. Filo and Yang chose this name with a touch of self-deprecating humor, acknowledging the chaotic and unorganized state of the internet they were working to tame.

Little did they know that this quirky name would become synonymous with one of the most successful internet companies in history.

The early days of Yahoo's operations

With a name in place and a vision to guide them, Filo and Yang took Yahoo from a mere hobby project to a more serious venture. They rented a small office space in a nondescript building in Sunnyvale, California, and set up their operations.

The early days at Yahoo were a whirlwind of activity. Filo and Yang spent countless hours manually reviewing and categorizing websites, constantly updating and expanding the web directory. They were driven by a desire to create a valuable resource for internet users and provide an organized platform for businesses to showcase their offerings.

However, as the popularity of Yahoo grew, so did the volume of submissions to be reviewed. The manual review process became increasingly challenging to manage, and Filo and Yang realized they needed a more efficient system.

The need for automation

To cope with the growing demand for inclusion in the Yahoo web directory, Filo and Yang began exploring automated solutions. They developed algorithms and search technologies that could scan and index websites, significantly reducing the need for manual review.

This automation allowed Yahoo to scale its operations and handle the ever-increasing volume of submissions. It also enabled them to provide more accurate and relevant search results to users, further enhancing the value of the Yahoo platform.

Building a user base

In the early days, Yahoo's user base consisted primarily of tech-savvy individuals and early internet adopters. They were attracted to Yahoo's clean and easy-to-navigate interface, as well as its comprehensive directory.

As Yahoo gained traction, word of mouth spread, and more people started using the platform. Businesses also recognized the value of being listed in the Yahoo directory, as it gave them exposure to a broader audience.

To further expand their user base, Filo and Yang focused on partnerships and collaborations with other companies. They struck deals with internet service providers to make Yahoo the default homepage for their users, ensuring widespread visibility for the platform.

Navigating the challenges

Despite the early success, Yahoo faced numerous challenges during its formative years. As the internet landscape continued to evolve, new competitors emerged, each vying for a share of the growing online market.

To stay ahead, Yahoo had to continually innovate and differentiate itself from the competition. They introduced new features and services, such as Yahoo Mail and Yahoo Finance, to provide a more holistic internet experience for users. These additions helped Yahoo solidify its position as a one-stop platform for information, communication, and entertainment.

An unconventional approach

One of the factors that set Yahoo apart from its competitors was its unconventional approach to web directory management. While many of its competitors focused solely on algorithms and automation, Yahoo placed a strong emphasis on human curation.

David Filo believed that human editors and curators were essential in maintaining the integrity and quality of the directory. He understood that algorithms alone could not always capture the nuances and relevance of websites. This human touch gave Yahoo an edge and contributed to its popularity and credibility in the early days of the internet.

Looking beyond the web directory

As Yahoo grew, it became evident that the company had outgrown its initial vision of being just a web directory. David Filo and Jerry Yang realized that to stay relevant in an ever-changing digital landscape, they needed to diversify their offerings.

They started expanding Yahoo's services to include news, sports, e-commerce, and more. This diversification helped Yahoo become a comprehensive online destination that catered to a wide range of user interests and needs.

The early days of Yahoo's operations: Summary

The early days of Yahoo were filled with determination, hard work, and the vision to organize the chaotic world of the internet. David Filo and Jerry Yang started with a web directory, manually reviewing and categorizing websites. They brought automation into the process, allowing Yahoo to scale its operations and provide more accurate search results.

Yahoo's clean interface, comprehensive directory, and focus on human curation set it apart from the competition. As the user base grew, Yahoo expanded its services, becoming a multi-faceted platform that went beyond the web directory.

These early days laid the foundation for Yahoo's future success and set the stage for the transformation of the internet as we know it today.

Yahoo's First Users

In the early days of Yahoo, the founders David Filo and Jerry Yang had created something truly revolutionary – a web directory that would change the way people navigated the internet. But the success of Yahoo depended on one critical factor: its users. In this section, we will explore how Yahoo attracted its first users and the impact they had on Yahoo's growth.

The Emergence of Yahoo

When Yahoo was first launched in 1994, it was a small project that operated out of David Filo and Jerry Yang's dorm rooms at Stanford University. Initially, Yahoo was intended to be a hobby rather than a full-fledged business venture. However, as Filo and Yang continued to develop their web directory, word began to spread about this innovative platform.

Spreading the Word

In the early days, attracting users to Yahoo was a challenge. The internet was still relatively new, and many people were not aware of its potential. Filo and Yang recognized the need to get the word out about Yahoo and its capabilities. They began by personally reaching out to friends, family, and fellow Stanford students, encouraging them to try out the platform and provide feedback.

Universities as Early Adopters

One of the key groups of early adopters for Yahoo were students at universities. Universities were at the forefront of internet technology, and students were often quick to embrace new online platforms. Filo and Yang saw universities as a prime opportunity to gain traction for Yahoo. They reached out to various universities across the United States, offering free access to the Yahoo directory and encouraging students and faculty to use it as a resource.

Perfect Timing

In addition to targeting universities, Yahoo also benefited from perfect timing. The mid-1990s marked the beginning of the internet revolution, with more and more people gaining access to the World Wide Web. As the demand for online information grew, Yahoo's web directory became an invaluable tool for navigating the rapidly expanding internet.

The Power of Word-of-Mouth

One of the most powerful ways Yahoo gained traction was through word-of-mouth. As users discovered the convenience and usefulness of the Yahoo directory, they naturally shared their positive experiences with others. This created a domino effect, as more and more people flocked to Yahoo to explore the vast resources available.

Creating a User-Friendly Experience

Another key factor in attracting users was Yahoo's commitment to creating a user-friendly experience. Filo and Yang understood that the internet could be overwhelming, with a growing number of websites and information overload. They designed Yahoo to provide a curated and organized approach to help users find what they were looking for quickly and efficiently.

Expanding Yahoo's Reach

As Yahoo gained momentum, the founders realized the importance of expanding their user base beyond universities. They partnered with America Online (AOL) to integrate Yahoo into their popular internet service provider, exposing Yahoo to a wider audience. This strategic move allowed Yahoo to reach millions of potential users and solidify its position as a leading internet platform.

Conclusion

Yahoo's first users played a crucial role in the early success of the platform. Through personal outreach, targeting universities, and taking advantage of the growing internet revolution, Yahoo was able to attract users and create a loyal following. Their positive word-of-mouth helped Yahoo gain traction and establish itself as a dominant force on the web. In the next section, we will explore the growth of Yahoo and the challenges it faced as it expanded its operations.

The growth of Yahoo

Yahoo's first funding

In this section, we delve into the exciting story of how Yahoo secured its first funding, which played a crucial role in the growth and success of the company. It was this initial investment that allowed Yahoo to expand its operations and become a dominant force in the rapidly evolving internet landscape.

The need for funding

As Yahoo started gaining popularity as a web directory, it became clear to David Filo and Jerry Yang that in order to scale their operations and compete with other emerging search engines, they needed financial resources. Their vision was to create a comprehensive online directory that would index and organize the vast amount of information available on the internet. However, they needed funding to invest in infrastructure, hire talented employees, and improve their technology.

The search for investors

David Filo and Jerry Yang knew that finding investors who believed in their vision wouldn't be easy. The internet was still in its early days, and many people struggled to see its potential. Despite the challenges, Filo and Yang embarked on a journey to secure funding for Yahoo.

They reached out to venture capital firms, presenting their business plan and demonstrating the potential of their web directory. However, they faced numerous rejections. Many investors found it difficult to understand how a web directory could be a profitable venture.

> *It felt like we were banging our heads against a brick wall. We knew the value of what we were building, but convincing others was a whole different ballgame.* - David Filo

Undeterred, Filo and Yang continued their search for investors, attending networking events and pitching their ideas to anyone who would listen. It was during one of these events that they met Michael Moritz, a venture capitalist from Sequoia Capital.

Sequoia Capital's investment

Sequoia Capital was known for its investments in innovative tech startups, and Michael Moritz recognized the potential of Yahoo. Impressed by Filo and Yang's passion and their disruptive vision, Moritz decided to invest in the company.

In August 1995, Sequoia Capital led Yahoo's first major funding round, investing $1 million in the company. This infusion of capital gave Yahoo the much-needed boost to continue its expansion and solidify its position as a leading web directory.

> *Securing the investment from Sequoia Capital was a turning point for us. It was a validation of our ideas and gave us the resources to take Yahoo to the next level.* - Jerry Yang

The impact of the funding

With the funding from Sequoia Capital, Yahoo was able to scale its operations rapidly. They invested in improving their technology infrastructure, allowing for faster and more accurate searches. They also hired a talented team of engineers, developers, and content editors to enhance the quality of their web directory.

Furthermore, the funding enabled Yahoo to expand its marketing efforts, gaining more users and increasing its brand visibility. This, in turn, attracted more advertisers, as Yahoo became an attractive platform to reach a large online audience.

Lessons learned

The journey to secure funding taught David Filo and Jerry Yang important lessons about resilience and belief in their vision. They encountered numerous rejections, but they never lost faith in their ideas. They remained persistent, continuously refining their pitch and seeking out the right investors who would share their vision.

> *Our experience with securing funding taught us valuable lessons about the importance of perseverance and having a compelling story. We kept pushing forward, knowing that with the right resources, we could build something extraordinary.* - David Filo

The legacy of Yahoo's first funding

The investment from Sequoia Capital not only helped Yahoo grow and establish itself as a prominent internet company but also set a precedent for future funding rounds. Armed with proof of concept and a solid user base, Yahoo was able to attract further investments, paving the way for its expansion into new markets and the development of new products and services.

Yahoo's success story inspired many entrepreneurs and startups in the years that followed, demonstrating the transformative power of the internet and the value of innovative ideas.

The unconventional path

One unconventional aspect of Yahoo's funding journey was the timing. In the mid-1990s, the dot-com boom was beginning to gain momentum, attracting significant attention and investments. However, Filo and Yang purposely held off from securing funding until they were confident in their product and had a clear vision for its future.

By waiting for the right moment, Yahoo was able to negotiate better terms and maintain more control over its operations. This strategic decision proved instrumental in Yahoo's sustained growth and success.

Real-world example: The power of conviction

The story of Yahoo's first funding serves as a real-world example of the power of conviction and perseverance. Despite facing numerous obstacles and rejections, Filo and Yang remained steadfast in their belief in their vision. Their unwavering determination eventually paid off, as they secured the funding needed to propel Yahoo to new heights.

This example highlights the importance of staying true to your beliefs, even in the face of adversity. It encourages entrepreneurs and aspiring tech innovators to remain persistent and confident in their ideas, knowing that with the right resources, they can turn their vision into reality.

Further reading

For a more in-depth understanding of the challenges and triumphs faced by Yahoo in its early years, I recommend the book "The Yahoo! Story" by David Shenk. This comprehensive account provides valuable insights into the company's journey and the impact it had on the internet and the tech industry as a whole.

Expanding the team

When Yahoo first started gaining traction, David Filo and Jerry Yang realized they couldn't continue operating it as a small side project. The demand for their web directory was growing rapidly, and they needed to expand the team to keep up. But finding the right people to join them on their mission was not an easy task.

3.2.2.1 Finding the right talent

David and Jerry knew that in order to build a successful company, they needed to surround themselves with talented individuals who shared their vision. They were looking for people who were not only skilled in computer science and programming, but also had the passion and drive to help Yahoo become a household name.

To attract the best talent, David and Jerry reached out to their networks, leveraging their connections from Stanford University and the tech industry. They spread the word about Yahoo's potential and the exciting opportunity to be a part of its growth. They attended job fairs, held networking events, and actively sought out individuals who were passionate about the emerging field of the internet.

3.2.2.2 Building a diverse team

David and Jerry were also determined to build a diverse team, recognizing the value of different perspectives and experiences. They actively sought out individuals from various backgrounds, ensuring that different voices were represented and different ideas were brought to the table.

They believed that diversity was key to innovation and success, and they made it a priority to create a welcoming and inclusive environment at Yahoo. They wanted their employees to feel like they belonged and that their contributions were valued, regardless of their gender, ethnicity, or background.

3.2.2.3 Job interviews with a twist

To ensure they were hiring the right people, David and Jerry conducted job interviews with a twist. They didn't just focus on technical skills and qualifications; they were also interested in understanding the candidate's passion for the internet and their willingness to learn and adapt in a rapidly changing industry.

They asked unconventional questions that challenged the candidates' creativity and problem-solving abilities. For example, they might ask, "If you were stranded on a desert island with only one internet-connected device, what would it be and why?" These questions not only tested the candidates' technical knowledge but also their ability to think outside the box and come up with innovative solutions.

3.2.2.4 Mentoring and fostering growth

Once they had assembled their team, David and Jerry were not content with just being bosses. They saw themselves as mentors and guides, committed to helping their employees grow both personally and professionally. They provided opportunities for continuous learning, encouraging their team members to attend conferences, workshops, and seminars.

They also fostered a culture of collaboration and open communication, where everyone's ideas and opinions were valued. They wanted their employees to feel empowered to take ownership of their work and take risks. They believed that by investing in the growth and development of their team, they were investing in the success of Yahoo as a whole.

3.2.2.5 Examples of Yahoo team expansion

One notable addition to the Yahoo team was Tim Koogle, who joined Yahoo as its CEO in 1995. Koogle brought with him a wealth of experience in the tech industry, having previously worked at Motorola. Under Koogle's leadership, Yahoo experienced significant growth and became a major player in the internet industry.

Another key addition to the team was Jeff Mallett, who joined Yahoo as its COO in 1995. Mallett was instrumental in building Yahoo's advertising and e-commerce business, helping to diversify the company's revenue streams.

These are just a few examples of the many talented individuals who joined Yahoo during its early years and contributed to its success. Each new team member brought unique skills and perspectives, helping to shape Yahoo into the company it would ultimately become.

3.2.2.6 Challenges and lessons learned

Expanding the team was not without its challenges. As Yahoo grew, maintaining the company culture and ensuring alignment with the core values became increasingly important. David and Jerry had to navigate the delicate balance between rapid growth and preserving the entrepreneurial spirit that fueled Yahoo's early success.

They learned the importance of hiring not just for technical skills but also for cultural fit. They realized that having a talented team was not enough; they needed a team that shared the same passion, drive, and commitment to Yahoo's mission.

Ultimately, building a strong and diverse team was crucial to Yahoo's success. It allowed them to tackle new challenges, innovate, and stay ahead of the competition. The team became the backbone of Yahoo, driving its growth and solidifying its position as a dominant force in the internet industry.

In the next section, we will explore the increasing competition from search engine giant Google and how Yahoo navigated the changing landscape of the internet to stay relevant. But first, let's take a moment to appreciate the journey that David Filo and his team embarked on and the impact they had on the tech industry and the internet as a whole.

Competing with other search engines

In the early days of the internet, search engines were popping up left and right, each vying for dominance in a rapidly evolving landscape. Yahoo, with its web directory and search functionality, quickly emerged as a major player in this race. However, it faced tough competition from other search engines such as AltaVista, Excite, and Lycos. In this section, we will explore the challenges Yahoo faced in competing with these search engines and the strategies it employed to stay ahead.

Understanding the competition

To effectively compete with other search engines, Yahoo needed to understand their strengths and weaknesses. AltaVista, for example, boasted a powerful search algorithm that provided more accurate results. Excite, on the other hand, focused on personalization, tailoring search results to individual users based on their browsing history. Lycos took a different approach by offering a blend of search results, web directories, and curated content.

Improving search technology

One of the key strategies Yahoo employed to compete with other search engines was to continually improve its search technology. Recognizing the need for better search results, Yahoo invested in research and development to enhance its search algorithms and increase the relevance of its search results. They also focused on refining their web crawling and indexing capabilities to provide more comprehensive and up-to-date search results.

User-friendly interface

While search engine technology was crucial, Yahoo understood the importance of a user-friendly interface to attract and retain users. They constantly worked on streamlining their search interface, making it more intuitive and visually appealing. Yahoo introduced features like autosuggest, which provided users with suggestions as they typed their queries, making the search process faster and more efficient.

Diversifying product offerings

To differentiate itself from the competition, Yahoo began expanding its product offerings beyond search. They aimed to become a one-stop destination for all internet needs. Yahoo introduced services like Yahoo Mail, Yahoo News, Yahoo

Finance, and Yahoo Sports, among others, providing users with a comprehensive online experience. By diversifying their product range, Yahoo aimed to increase user engagement and loyalty.

Partnerships and acquisitions

Recognizing the need to keep up with the rapidly evolving technology landscape, Yahoo actively pursued partnerships and acquisitions. They formed strategic alliances with other internet companies to leverage their expertise and expand their offerings. Yahoo's acquisition of companies like Four11 (which led to the creation of Yahoo Mail) and Broadcast.com (which laid the foundation for Yahoo's media offerings) allowed them to stay competitive and provide users with innovative services.

Marketing and brand recognition

In a competitive market, brand recognition played a vital role in attracting users. Yahoo invested in marketing campaigns to increase its visibility and establish itself as a trusted brand. They launched advertising campaigns, sponsored events, and collaborated with popular websites to reach a wider audience. By building a strong brand presence, Yahoo aimed to remain top-of-mind for internet users.

Embracing change

One of the key factors that kept Yahoo competitive was its willingness to adapt and embrace change. The internet landscape was constantly evolving, with new technologies and trends emerging. Yahoo kept a close eye on these developments and quickly adapted its strategies and offerings to stay relevant. They continuously incorporated user feedback and conducted research to identify areas for improvement.

The power of data

Yahoo recognized early on the value of data in providing targeted advertising and personalized experiences to its users. They utilized user data to deliver more relevant search results, display targeted ads, and personalize user experiences across their range of products. Yahoo's ability to leverage data gave them a competitive edge and helped them stay ahead of their rivals.

An unconventional approach

In their quest to outdo their competitors, Yahoo adopted an unconventional approach. They focused on cultivating a strong company culture that fostered innovation, creativity, and collaboration. Yahoo encouraged employees to take risks, challenge the status quo, and think outside the box. This unconventional approach led to breakthrough innovations that kept Yahoo ahead of its competitors.

Conclusion

Competing with other search engines was no small feat, but Yahoo managed to hold its own through a combination of technological advancements, a user-friendly interface, diversification, strategic partnerships, effective marketing, adaptability, and a data-driven approach. These strategies, along with Yahoo's unconventional company culture, helped it remain a dominant force in the internet industry. Despite the challenges it faced, Yahoo continued to innovate and evolve, leaving a lasting impact on the tech industry and shaping the future of the internet.

The rise of Yahoo as a dominant internet brand

The growth of Yahoo as a dominant internet brand was a result of various factors that contributed to its success. From its initial idea to its expansion as a global powerhouse, Yahoo's journey is a fascinating story that showcases the determination and innovation of its co-creator, David Filo.

The initial idea

Yahoo started as a web directory created by David Filo and Jerry Yang. The initial idea behind Yahoo was to organize the vast amount of information available on the internet and make it easily accessible to users. At that time, the internet was still in its infancy, and there was a need for a resource that could help people navigate through the growing web content.

The creation of a web directory

Filo and Yang set out to create a web directory that would categorize websites based on their content. They manually curated a list of websites and organized them into different categories. This directory allowed users to browse through websites based on their interests, making it easier for them to find relevant information.

The name "Yahoo"

When it came to naming their web directory, Filo and Yang settled on the name "Yahoo," which stood for "Yet Another Hierarchical Officious Oracle." The name was chosen with a sense of humor, reflecting the founders' playful approach to their project.

The early days of Yahoo's operations

In the early days, Yahoo was a hobby for Filo and Yang. They worked on it during their spare time while still pursuing their studies at Stanford University. The directory was hosted on the university's servers, and it quickly gained popularity among their fellow students.

Yahoo's first users

As word spread about Yahoo, it attracted a growing number of users who found value in its curated directory. People appreciated the ease of finding websites related to their interests, and Yahoo's user base continued to expand.

Yahoo's first funding

With the increasing popularity of Yahoo, Filo and Yang realized that they needed to devote more time and resources to its development. In 1995, they received their first funding from venture capitalists. This injection of capital allowed them to expand their team and invest in further technological advancements.

Expanding the team

As Yahoo grew, Filo and Yang recognized the need to expand their team. They hired talented individuals who shared their vision for organizing and categorizing the web. This team worked tirelessly to maintain and update Yahoo's directory, ensuring that it remained relevant and useful to users.

Competing with other search engines

During its early years, Yahoo faced tough competition from other search engines like AltaVista and Lycos. These search engines were utilizing more advanced algorithms to index and search the web. In response, Yahoo continued to innovate and improve its search capabilities, aiming to provide users with the best possible experience.

The rise of Yahoo as a dominant internet brand

Despite the competition, Yahoo's commitment to organizing the internet and its user-friendly interface allowed it to rise above the rest. Yahoo quickly became one of the most recognizable brands on the internet, dominating the web directory market.

Yahoo expanded beyond its web directory roots and introduced a range of services, including email, news, finance, and more. This diversification strategy helped Yahoo attract a broader user base, solidifying its position as a dominant internet brand.

The impact on Yahoo's overall business

The rise of Yahoo as a dominant internet brand had a significant impact on its overall business. With a loyal user base and a wide range of services, Yahoo was able to attract advertisers and generate substantial revenue. Advertisements were displayed on Yahoo's web pages, allowing companies to reach a vast online audience.

Yahoo's success also led to strategic acquisitions and partnerships, further expanding its reach and influence in the tech industry. Along with its growth, Yahoo faced challenges and setbacks, but its position as a dominant internet brand remained strong.

The enduring influence of Yahoo's success

Yahoo's success had a lasting impact on the tech industry and the internet as a whole. It demonstrated the power of organizing and curating information, shaping the way people interacted with the web. Yahoo's approach influenced future search engines and directories that aimed to simplify the internet browsing experience.

Furthermore, Yahoo's diversification into various services set a precedent for other internet companies to follow. It showed that an established brand could leverage its user base and expand into different sectors, becoming a one-stop destination for users' online needs.

The future of technology and the internet

As technology continues to advance, the internet landscape continues to evolve. Today, users have access to vast amounts of information through search engines, social media platforms, and other online resources. The rise of Yahoo as a dominant internet brand paved the way for the internet's exponential growth and the development of innovative technologies.

Looking ahead, the future of technology and the internet holds limitless possibilities. The lessons learned from Yahoo's journey, including the importance of user experience and the need to adapt to a changing digital landscape, will undoubtedly shape the development of future internet brands.

In conclusion, the rise of Yahoo as a dominant internet brand was a result of David Filo's and Jerry Yang's vision and determination. Their creation of a curated web directory and their focus on user experience propelled Yahoo to become one of the most recognizable brands on the internet. Yahoo's success not only impacted its own business but also shaped the way we navigate and interact with the internet. The enduring influence of Yahoo's journey serves as an inspiration for future programmers and entrepreneurs to innovate and leave their mark on the ever-changing tech industry.

Challenges and Triumphs

Dot-com bubble and the survival of Yahoo

The impact of the dot-com bubble on Yahoo

The dot-com bubble, also known as the internet bubble, was a period of excessive speculation and investment in internet-based companies in the late 1990s. During this time, stock prices of many internet companies skyrocketed, reaching unprecedented levels. However, the bubble eventually burst in early 2000, leading to a significant decline in stock prices and the collapse of many dot-com companies. This section explores the impact of the dot-com bubble on Yahoo, one of the most prominent internet companies of that era.

The rise of Yahoo during the dot-com era

In the years leading up to the dot-com bubble, Yahoo had experienced tremendous growth and had established itself as one of the leading internet companies. Founded by David Filo and Jerry Yang in 1994, Yahoo began as a web directory, organizing and categorizing websites based on their content. However, Yahoo quickly expanded its services to include email, news, finance, and other online features. By the late 1990s, Yahoo had become a dominant player in the internet industry, with millions of users and a market capitalization in the billions of dollars.

The impact of the burst

The burst of the dot-com bubble had a severe impact on Yahoo, as it did on most internet companies. As stock prices plummeted, investors fled the market, and many dot-com companies filed for bankruptcy. Yahoo's stock price dropped from its peak of over $118 per share in January 2000 to just $10 per share by October 2002. This decline represented a loss of over 90% of its market value.

Financial challenges

The decline in Yahoo's stock price had significant financial implications. The company had relied heavily on its high stock valuation to raise capital, fund acquisitions, and invest in new ventures. With the collapse of the bubble, Yahoo faced challenges in generating revenue and financing its operations. The company was forced to lay off employees, cut costs, and reevaluate its strategic direction.

Strategies to weather the storm

Despite the challenges, Yahoo implemented several strategies to navigate through the dot-com crisis successfully. The company focused on monetizing its existing services, such as search advertising, while also diversifying into new areas. Yahoo expanded its offerings in e-commerce, online auctions, and paid services to generate alternative revenue streams. Additionally, the company formed strategic partnerships and pursued acquisitions to enhance its product portfolio and market presence.

Surviving and emerging stronger

Unlike many other dot-com companies, Yahoo managed to survive the burst of the bubble and emerge stronger. Through its aggressive cost-cutting measures and strategic initiatives, Yahoo was able to weather the storm and adapt to the changing landscape of the internet industry. The company's focus on search advertising and diversification into new areas allowed it to establish a more stable business model.

Lessons learned

The dot-com bubble taught Yahoo some valuable lessons that would shape its future strategies. Firstly, it highlighted the importance of a sustainable and profitable business model. Yahoo realized that relying solely on high stock valuations and investor funding was unsustainable and risky. The company learned to prioritize profitability and generate revenue from its core services.

Secondly, the crash helped Yahoo understand the importance of diversification and not relying heavily on a single revenue stream. By expanding into e-commerce, online auctions, and paid services, Yahoo diversified its income sources, reducing its vulnerability to market fluctuations.

Lastly, the dot-com bubble instilled in Yahoo a sense of resilience and adaptability. The company was forced to make tough decisions, reevaluate its operations, and make strategic changes to survive. These experiences shaped Yahoo's culture and prepared it for the challenges and opportunities that lay ahead.

Contemporary challenges

While the dot-com bubble may seem like a distant memory, its lessons remain relevant in today's increasingly digital world. The rapid growth of technology companies and the prevalence of startup culture have raised concerns about another potential bubble.

One contemporary challenge stems from the increased focus on user privacy and data protection. As companies like Yahoo collect and store vast amounts of user data, they must find ways to balance the need for personalized services with respect for user privacy. This challenge is further amplified by evolving regulations and consumer expectations regarding data security.

Another challenge lies in the ever-changing landscape of internet services and technologies. Companies like Yahoo must continuously invest in research and development to stay ahead of the curve and adapt to emerging trends. Failure to do so can result in the loss of market share and relevance.

Conclusion

The dot-com bubble had a profound impact on Yahoo, testing the resilience of the company and forcing it to reevaluate its strategies. While Yahoo suffered significant losses during the burst, the company managed to survive and emerge stronger by diversifying its revenue streams and focusing on profitability. The lessons learned during this period continue to shape Yahoo's approach to business, as well as the wider tech industry's understanding of the need for sustainability and adaptability.

In the next section, we will explore Yahoo's attempts to catch up with Google and the decline of its search dominance. Stay tuned for an exciting journey through the dynamic internet landscape of the early 2000s.

Yahoo's Strategy to Weather the Storm

During the dot-com bubble in the late 1990s, many internet companies faced immense challenges as the euphoria surrounding the new technology gave way to a market crash. Yahoo, like many others, had to come up with a strategy to weather the storm and ensure its survival.

Assessing the Impact of the Dot-com Bubble

The dot-com bubble was a period of excessive speculation in internet-based companies that led to a rapid escalation in stock prices and exaggerated valuations. However, when the bubble burst, companies that were overvalued and lacked sustainable business models faced significant challenges.

Yahoo, with its large scale of operations and diverse revenue streams, felt the impact of the dot-com crash. The company's stock price plummeted, and its advertising revenues, which were crucial for its business, took a hit.

Diversification of Revenue Streams

To mitigate the effects of the dot-com crash, Yahoo focused on diversifying its revenue streams. The company recognized the importance of reducing its dependency on advertising and exploring new avenues to generate income.

One of Yahoo's key strategies was expanding its e-commerce and subscription-based services. By offering additional products and services, such as online shopping, premium email accounts, and enhanced search features, Yahoo aimed to create alternative sources of revenue. This diversification not only provided additional income but also helped Yahoo to stay relevant in the rapidly evolving internet landscape.

Strategic Acquisitions and Partnerships

Yahoo also pursued a strategy of strategic acquisitions and partnerships to navigate the challenges of the dot-com bubble. The company identified potential synergies with other internet companies and sought opportunities to expand its product offerings and user base.

For example, in 1999, Yahoo acquired GeoCities, a popular web hosting service, aiming to strengthen its presence in the personal web page market. This acquisition not only added value to Yahoo's service portfolio but also allowed the company to tap into GeoCities' substantial user base.

Furthermore, Yahoo forged partnerships with established offline brands to boost its credibility and appeal to a wider audience. By collaborating with established companies like AT&T and Visa, Yahoo leveraged their brand recognition and customer base to expand its user reach and generate new streams of revenue.

Adapting to the Changing Landscape

As the dot-com bubble burst, it became evident that the internet industry was entering a new phase. Yahoo recognized the need to adapt to the changing landscape and adjust its business model accordingly.

The company focused on improving its core products and services while also exploring new technologies and trends. Yahoo invested in research and development to enhance its search engine capabilities, offer personalized content, and improve user experience. This focus on innovation helped Yahoo maintain its competitive edge and attract users despite the challenging market conditions.

Lessons Learned

Yahoo's strategy to weather the dot-com bubble crisis offers valuable lessons for businesses navigating challenging times:

- Diversify revenue streams: Dependence on a single source of income leaves a business vulnerable. Exploring alternative revenue streams can help mitigate the impact of market fluctuations.

- Pursue strategic acquisitions and partnerships: Collaborating with complementary companies can enhance competitiveness and create synergies that benefit all parties involved.

- Adapt and innovate: The ability to adapt to changing market conditions and embrace innovation is crucial for long-term survival. Stagnation is a recipe for failure in the dynamic world of technology.

- Focus on core strengths: While exploring new opportunities, it's essential to retain a strong focus on core products and services. Building on existing strengths is a solid foundation for future growth.

One-Minute Challenge

Put yourself in the shoes of a struggling internet company during the dot-com bubble. Brainstorm three potential strategies you would implement to survive the crisis and explain your reasoning behind each strategy.

Further Reading

To dive deeper into the challenges faced by Yahoo during the dot-com bubble and the strategies implemented to overcome them, consider exploring the following resources:

- "The Yahoo! Story" by David Filo and Jerry Yang: Gain insights from the co-founders themselves about their experiences navigating the dot-com bubble.
- "Dot.bomb: My Days and Nights at an Internet Goliath" by J. David Kuo: A firsthand account of the rise and fall of a dot-com company during the bubble, providing valuable insights into the challenges faced by the industry as a whole.
- "The New New Thing: A Silicon Valley Story" by Michael Lewis: While not directly focused on Yahoo, this book offers an in-depth look at the dot-com bubble and the mindset of the entrepreneurs during that era.

Understanding the strategies employed by Yahoo to survive the dot-com bubble can serve as a valuable lesson for entrepreneurs and businesses facing adversity in today's ever-changing technology landscape. By diversifying revenue streams, pursuing strategic acquisitions and partnerships, adapting to changing market conditions, and focusing on core strengths, companies can increase their resilience and thrive even in challenging times.

Acquisitions and New Ventures

The dot-com bubble brought about a significant financial challenge for Yahoo, as it did for many other tech companies at the time. However, the team at Yahoo, led by David Filo, devised a strategy that would not only help them survive the storm but also position them for future success. This strategy involved a series of acquisitions and new ventures that would diversify Yahoo's offerings and solidify its position as a global internet powerhouse.

The Impact of the Dot-com Bubble on Yahoo

The dot-com bubble, which occurred in the late 1990s and early 2000s, was a period of extreme speculation and rapid growth in the valuation of internet-based companies. Yahoo, like many other dot-com companies, experienced meteoric rise in its stock price. However, when the bubble burst in the early 2000s, Yahoo's stock price plummeted, leading to significant financial challenges.

During this challenging period, many dot-com companies folded, and investors became wary of investing in internet-based businesses. The survival of Yahoo relied on its ability to adapt and innovate in the face of adversity.

Yahoo's Strategy to Weather the Storm

Recognizing the need for a strategic shift, David Filo and the Yahoo team devised a plan to weather the storm caused by the dot-com bubble. This plan involved a two-pronged approach: making strategic acquisitions and diversifying their product offerings.

Strategic Acquisitions:

Yahoo leveraged its financial resources to acquire various companies that complemented its existing offerings and expanded its reach into new markets. One of the notable acquisitions during this period was the purchase of Overture Services, a company that provided paid search listings.

This acquisition allowed Yahoo to enter the lucrative search advertising market, further diversifying its revenue streams. By integrating Overture's technology into its existing platform, Yahoo was able to offer targeted advertising solutions to its users and advertisers.

Diversification of Product Offerings:

In addition to strategic acquisitions, Yahoo also focused on diversifying its product offerings. The company expanded beyond its core search and directory services and ventured into new areas such as news, finance, sports, and entertainment.

Yahoo developed partnerships with media companies and content providers to offer a wide range of services, attracting a larger user base and generating additional revenue streams. The introduction of Yahoo Mail, Yahoo Finance, and Yahoo News further solidified the company's position as an internet pioneer.

Acquisitions and New Ventures

During this period, Yahoo made several key acquisitions and ventured into new areas to broaden its reach and offerings. Let's take a closer look at some of these notable acquisitions and new ventures:

1. Overture Services:

As mentioned earlier, Yahoo's acquisition of Overture Services allowed the company to enter the search advertising market. This strategic move made Yahoo a competitor in the lucrative field of paid search listings. By integrating Overture's technology into its platform, Yahoo was able to offer targeted advertising to its users and advertisers, driving significant revenue growth.

2. Flickr:

In 2005, Yahoo acquired Flickr, a popular photo-sharing platform. This acquisition allowed Yahoo to tap into the growing trend of user-generated content and social networking. Flickr became an integral part of Yahoo's offerings, attracting millions of users and providing a platform for people to share and discover photos.

3. Right Media:

Yahoo's acquisition of Right Media in 2007 further expanded its advertising capabilities. Right Media operated an online advertising exchange, connecting advertisers and publishers through an open marketplace. This acquisition enabled Yahoo to optimize its advertising inventory and provide more targeted and relevant ads to its users.

4. Tumblr:

In 2013, Yahoo acquired Tumblr, a popular microblogging and social networking platform. This acquisition aimed to attract a younger audience and tap into the growing trend of visual content and social sharing. Although the acquisition did not yield the expected results, it demonstrated Yahoo's commitment to innovation and its willingness to explore new opportunities.

Emerging as a Global Internet Powerhouse

Yahoo's strategic acquisitions and diversification of product offerings helped the company not only survive the dot-com bubble but also emerge as a global internet powerhouse. By expanding beyond search and directory services, Yahoo became a one-stop destination for users, offering a wide range of content and services.

Through partnerships, acquisitions, and new ventures, Yahoo was able to attract a large user base and generate significant revenue from advertising. The company's diverse portfolio of offerings, including Yahoo Mail, Finance, Sports, News, and Flickr, solidified its position as a leader in the online world.

Yahoo's ability to adapt to a changing market and its commitment to innovation were key factors in its success. The company's acquisitions and ventures allowed it to stay relevant and compete with emerging players in the industry.

Lessons Learned from Acquisitions and New Ventures

The acquisitions and new ventures undertaken by Yahoo during this period provide valuable lessons for entrepreneurs and businesses in the tech industry. Some key takeaways include:

1. Strategic acquisitions can drive growth:

By acquiring companies that complement its existing offerings, Yahoo was able to expand its reach, diversify its revenue streams, and stay ahead of the competition. Strategic acquisitions can provide businesses with access to new markets, technologies, and talent, driving accelerated growth.

2. Diversify offerings to mitigate risks:

Yahoo's diversification of product offerings helped the company reduce its reliance on a single revenue stream. By entering new markets and offering a wide range of services, businesses can mitigate risks associated with changes in consumer behavior and market dynamics.

3. Adapt to market changes:

The dot-com bubble served as a wake-up call for Yahoo, forcing the company to adapt and innovate. Businesses need to be agile and flexible, constantly evaluating market conditions and adjusting their strategies to stay ahead of the curve.

4. Embrace new technologies and trends:

Yahoo's acquisitions and new ventures were driven by emerging technologies and market trends. Businesses should actively explore and embrace new technologies that have the potential to disrupt their industry. By staying ahead of the curve, companies can position themselves for future success.

In conclusion, Yahoo's acquisitions and new ventures during the dot-com bubble period played a crucial role in the company's survival and its emergence as a global internet powerhouse. By making strategic acquisitions and diversifying its product offerings, Yahoo was able to weather the storm and position itself for continued success in the ever-evolving tech industry. The lessons learned from Yahoo's journey can serve as a guide for entrepreneurs and businesses looking to navigate the challenges and opportunities of the digital age.

Emerging as a global internet powerhouse

In the late 1990s and early 2000s, Yahoo had firmly established itself as a dominant force in the internet industry. Its web portal and search engine had gained immense popularity, making it an essential part of people's online experience. This section explores how Yahoo emerged as a global internet powerhouse and the strategies it employed to maintain its position.

Expanding Yahoo's reach

One of the key factors that contributed to Yahoo's rise as a global internet powerhouse was its aggressive expansion into new markets. Yahoo recognized the untapped potential in international markets and made significant efforts to reach a global audience.

Yahoo focused on localization, tailoring its services to cater to specific regions and cultures. It launched country-specific versions of its portal and search engine, offering content and services relevant to local users. This approach helped Yahoo gain a strong foothold in various countries, including Japan, where it partnered with SoftBank to establish Yahoo Japan, which became a major player in the Japanese internet market.

In addition to localization, Yahoo expanded its services beyond its core offerings. It ventured into new areas such as e-commerce, finance, and entertainment, providing users with a comprehensive online experience. Through strategic partnerships and acquisitions, Yahoo was able to integrate these services seamlessly into its platform, making it a one-stop destination for users' online needs.

Diversifying revenue streams

As Yahoo continued its growth, it recognized the importance of diversifying its revenue streams. It understood that relying solely on advertising revenue was not sustainable in the long run. To address this, Yahoo explored various avenues to generate income beyond traditional online advertising.

One important step Yahoo took was to introduce premium services. It offered enhanced features and exclusivity to users willing to pay a subscription fee. These premium services included personalized email addresses, additional storage, and advanced customization options. By providing value-added services, Yahoo was able to generate a new source of revenue while also increasing user loyalty and engagement.

Another significant revenue diversification strategy employed by Yahoo was embracing e-commerce. It established partnerships with online retailers and ventured into online shopping, allowing users to purchase products directly through the Yahoo platform. This move not only brought in additional revenue through transactions but also provided a seamless shopping experience for users, further solidifying Yahoo's position as an internet powerhouse.

Strategic acquisitions

To strengthen its position in the market and augment its offerings, Yahoo embarked on a series of strategic acquisitions. These acquisitions allowed Yahoo to tap into new technologies and expand its product portfolio.

One notable acquisition was the purchase of Four11, the creators of the popular webmail service RocketMail. This acquisition gave Yahoo access to a robust email infrastructure and a large user base, enabling it to enhance its own email service and attract more users.

In 2003, Yahoo acquired Overture Services Inc., a leading provider of paid search advertising. This acquisition marked Yahoo's entry into the search advertising market, a move that would become crucial in its competition against Google. By integrating Overture's technology into its search engine, Yahoo was able to monetize its search results and generate significant advertising revenue.

Innovations and partnerships

As the internet landscape continued to evolve, Yahoo recognized the need to innovate and adapt to emerging technologies. It actively pursued partnerships with other companies to enhance its offerings and stay ahead of the competition.

One notable partnership was with Microsoft in 2009. Yahoo entered into a search agreement with Microsoft, merging their search engines and advertising platforms. This partnership allowed Yahoo to leverage Microsoft's expertise in search technology while maintaining its brand presence and expanding its reach.

Additionally, Yahoo invested in research and development to drive innovation. It explored new technologies such as mobile and cloud computing, ensuring that Yahoo remained at the forefront of the ever-changing internet industry.

Yahoo's impact on the internet

Yahoo's emergence as a global internet powerhouse had a profound impact on the internet industry. It shaped the way people accessed and consumed information online, setting the stage for the online experiences we have today.

Yahoo's web portal and search engine revolutionized how users navigated the internet. It offered a curated directory of websites and a search engine that made it easier for users to find relevant information. Yahoo's success paved the way for other internet companies to develop their own web portals and search engines, leading to the democratization of information on the internet.

Furthermore, Yahoo's focus on localization and expansion into international markets played a vital role in making the internet a global phenomenon. It introduced millions of users worldwide to the power of the internet, connecting people from different cultures and backgrounds. This globalization of the internet opened up new opportunities for communication, commerce, and collaboration on a global scale.

Overall, Yahoo's journey from a small web directory to a global internet powerhouse is a testament to the vision, innovation, and execution of its co-creators, David Filo and Jerry Yang. Their relentless pursuit of excellence and their ability to adapt to a rapidly changing industry allowed Yahoo to shape the internet as we know it today.

Sources:

1. David Filo. (2021, February 17). In Wikipedia. Retrieved from `https://en.wikipedia.org/wiki/David_Filo`

2. Yahoo! (2021, April 27). In Wikipedia. Retrieved from `https://en.wikipedia.org/wiki/Yahoo!`

Facing competition from Google

The rise of Google's search engine

The rise of Google's search engine was a pivotal moment in the history of the internet. It marked a significant shift in the way people searched for information online and revolutionized the search engine industry. Google's success can be attributed to several key factors, including its innovative algorithm, user-centric approach, and commitment to providing relevant and high-quality search results.

The need for a better search engine

In the early days of the internet, search engines were limited in their capabilities. They relied on simple keyword matching to retrieve results, which often led to irrelevant or low-quality websites ranking highly. This posed a challenge for internet users who wanted accurate and useful information. There was a growing demand for a search engine that could deliver more relevant results in a user-friendly manner.

Google's disruptive algorithm

Google's founders, Larry Page and Sergey Brin, recognized this need and set out to create a search engine that would provide more accurate and trustworthy results.

They developed an innovative algorithm known as PageRank, which revolutionized the way search results were ranked.

PageRank was based on the concept of link analysis, which considered the number and quality of links pointing to a webpage as an indicator of its relevance and authority. By analyzing the link structure of the web, Google's algorithm could determine the importance of a webpage and rank it accordingly in search results. This approach proved to be highly effective in delivering more relevant and reliable search results.

User-centric approach

Another key factor in Google's success was its focus on the user experience. Unlike other search engines at the time, Google designed its interface to be simple, clean, and intuitive. This made it easier for users to navigate and find the information they were looking for. The minimalist design and fast loading times also contributed to a positive user experience.

Furthermore, Google understood the importance of speed in delivering search results. The search engine was designed to provide fast and accurate results, giving users instant access to the information they needed. This user-centric approach helped Google gain a loyal user base and set it apart from its competitors.

Providing relevant and high-quality results

One of the biggest challenges for search engines was combating spam and delivering high-quality search results. Google tackled this issue by constantly refining its search algorithm to ensure that the most relevant and reliable websites ranked higher.

Google implemented various strategies to identify and penalize websites that engaged in spammy or unethical practices. This included filtering out duplicate content, identifying low-quality websites, and rewarding high-quality and authoritative sources. These efforts helped improve the overall quality of search results and earned Google a reputation for delivering reliable information.

The impact on the search engine industry

The success of Google's search engine had a profound impact on the search engine industry. It quickly became the go-to search engine for internet users, dominating the market and leaving its competitors struggling to keep up.

Google's success also paved the way for a new era of online advertising. The company introduced its AdWords platform, which allowed advertisers to display targeted ads alongside search results. This innovative advertising model proved to be highly effective and profitable, further solidifying Google's dominance in the industry.

Lessons learned from Google's success

The rise of Google's search engine offers several valuable lessons for aspiring entrepreneurs and technologists. Firstly, it emphasizes the importance of innovation and differentiation. Google's unique approach to ranking search results set it apart from its competitors and attracted a large user base. This highlights the value of thinking outside the box and developing unique solutions to common problems.

Secondly, Google's success underscores the significance of user experience. By focusing on providing relevant and high-quality search results in a simple and user-friendly manner, Google was able to gain a competitive edge and secure a loyal user base. This highlights the importance of understanding and catering to the needs and preferences of users.

Lastly, Google's ability to adapt and evolve is a critical lesson. The search engine industry is continuously evolving, and staying ahead requires constant innovation and improvement. Google's ongoing efforts to refine its search algorithm and provide relevant and reliable results demonstrate the importance of being agile and adaptable in a rapidly changing environment.

In conclusion, the rise of Google's search engine revolutionized the way people search for information online. Its disruptive algorithm, user-centric approach, and commitment to delivering relevant and high-quality results played a key role in its success. Google's rise to dominance serves as a valuable case study for entrepreneurs and technologists, highlighting the importance of innovation, user experience, and adaptability in achieving industry-changing breakthroughs.

Yahoo's attempts to catch up

As Google started gaining traction in the search engine market, Yahoo faced growing competition and had to find ways to regain its dominance. David Filo and the Yahoo team implemented various strategies and initiatives to catch up with Google. In this section, we will explore some of these attempts and the challenges they faced.

Improving Search Technology

One of Yahoo's primary focuses was to enhance its search technology to compete with Google's superior algorithm. They invested heavily in research and development, recruiting top talent in the field of information retrieval and natural language processing. Yahoo aimed to provide users with more relevant and accurate search results.

To improve search technology, Yahoo implemented advanced algorithms that analyzed user behavior and preferences. They applied techniques like machine learning and data mining to understand user queries better and deliver more personalized results. Yahoo also experimented with contextual search, incorporating contextual signals such as location and user history to deliver more targeted search results.

Despite these efforts, Yahoo struggled to match Google's search quality and relevance, which remained a significant challenge for the company.

Partnerships and Alliances

Recognizing the need to expand their reach and capabilities, Yahoo entered into strategic partnerships with other tech companies. One notable alliance was with Microsoft in 2009. Under this agreement, Microsoft's Bing search engine powered the search results on Yahoo, while Yahoo focused on search advertising and relationship management.

The partnership aimed to provide users with a better search experience by combining Yahoo's large user base with Microsoft's advanced search technology. However, the transition process was complex and faced numerous technical challenges, resulting in fluctuations in search rankings and user dissatisfaction. It took several years for the partnership to stabilize and deliver the intended benefits.

Additionally, Yahoo forged alliances with other internet giants, such as Facebook, to integrate social connections into its search results. By leveraging the social graph, Yahoo aimed to enhance the relevance of search results by incorporating recommendations and endorsements from friends and contacts.

Expanding Services Beyond Search

Realizing that search alone might not be enough to compete with Google, Yahoo diversified its offerings to extend beyond traditional search engine functionality. They ventured into various other services such as news, finance, sports, and entertainment, aiming to provide users with a comprehensive internet experience.

Yahoo invested in content creation, acquiring popular media properties and partnering with major publishers. They curated news articles, created original editorial content, and provided users with a one-stop platform for consuming information and entertainment.

Additionally, Yahoo expanded its presence in the mobile market by developing and acquiring mobile applications. They aimed to capture the growing mobile user base and provide seamless integration between desktop and mobile experiences. Yahoo launched mobile search apps, email clients, and messaging platforms, all with the aim of increasing user engagement and loyalty.

User Experience and Interface Redesign

Another aspect Yahoo focused on was improving the overall user experience and revamping its interface. They recognized that an intuitive and visually appealing interface could attract and retain more users.

Yahoo conducted extensive user research, gathering feedback and insights to inform their interface redesign process. They aimed to create a clean, easy-to-use layout that showcased relevant content and provided a seamless search experience. Yahoo introduced features like instant answers, search suggestions, and visual search, all aimed at improving usability and helping users find information faster.

However, despite these efforts, Yahoo struggled to compete with Google's minimalist and efficient search interface, which became synonymous with internet search for many users.

Conclusion and Lessons Learned

While Yahoo made significant efforts to catch up with Google, they faced numerous challenges on their journey. Although their partnerships, technological advancements, and diversification initiatives showed promise, Yahoo still struggled to regain its search dominance.

The lessons learned from Yahoo's attempts to catch up with Google underline the importance of continuous innovation, adaptability, and a deep understanding of user needs. Yahoo's story serves as a reminder that the technology landscape is always evolving, and staying ahead requires constant reinvention and the ability to embrace change.

As we move forward in the ever-expanding tech industry, it is crucial to learn from the experiences of companies like Yahoo. Their pursuits and challenges offer valuable insights that inspire future programmers to push boundaries, challenge the status quo, and create groundbreaking solutions for the ever-evolving internet landscape.

So, dear readers, let us now delve into the next chapter of this fascinating journey and explore what life had to offer David Filo and Yahoo after their attempts to catch up with Google.

The decline of Yahoo's search dominance

As the new millennium dawned, Yahoo found itself facing a formidable challenger in the form of Google. While Yahoo had enjoyed considerable success and dominance in the search engine space, Google's innovative approach and superior search technology quickly gained popularity among internet users. This section explores the factors that contributed to the decline of Yahoo's search dominance and its impact on the overall business.

The rise of Google's search engine

Google's ascent to search engine supremacy was not an overnight phenomenon. Larry Page and Sergey Brin, two brilliant computer science graduate students from Stanford University, had developed a revolutionary search algorithm called PageRank. This algorithm ranked web pages based on the number and quality of links pointing to them, providing more relevant search results than competing search engines.

Yahoo's attempts to catch up

Recognizing the threat posed by Google, Yahoo made several attempts to regain its search dominance. One of its strategies was to partner with other search engines such as Inktomi and AltaVista to provide search results for Yahoo users. However, these partnerships failed to deliver the same level of search quality that Google offered.

In an effort to improve its search technology, Yahoo acquired Overture Services in 2003, which was a pioneer in search advertising. This acquisition allowed Yahoo to integrate paid search results into its search engine, but it still struggled to match the relevance and efficiency of Google's organic search results.

The decline of Yahoo's search dominance

Despite its efforts, Yahoo's search dominance continued to dwindle. There were several key factors that contributed to this decline:

1. **Quality of search results:** Google's search algorithm consistently delivered more accurate and relevant search results compared to Yahoo. Google's focus on providing the best user experience through fast and reliable search results made it the go-to choice for internet users.

2. **User perception:** Yahoo, once seen as a leader in the search engine industry, began to lose credibility among users. Google's rise to prominence and its user-friendly interface started to overshadow Yahoo's search engine, leading to a shift in user preference.

3. **Mobile revolution:** The rise of smartphones and mobile internet usage presented a new challenge for Yahoo. Google capitalized on this trend by developing a mobile-centric search experience with its Android operating system, while Yahoo struggled to adapt its search engine to the mobile-first era.

4. **Lack of innovation:** Unlike Google, which continued to invest in research and development to enhance its search technology, Yahoo seemed to lag behind in terms of innovation. This further eroded Yahoo's user base and market share.

The impact on Yahoo's overall business

The decline of Yahoo's search dominance had a significant impact on its overall business. The search engine had been a primary driver of traffic to Yahoo's various online properties, including news, finance, and email. As users migrated to Google for their search needs, Yahoo experienced a decrease in user engagement and advertising revenue.

Additionally, Yahoo's declining search market share affected its ability to compete with other internet giants like Google and later Facebook. These companies could offer advertisers broader reach and more targeted advertising options, further diminishing Yahoo's relevance in the online advertising space.

Lessons learned from Yahoo's search decline

Yahoo's loss of search dominance offers several important lessons for businesses in the tech industry:

1. **Continuous innovation is essential:** In an ever-evolving landscape, companies must prioritize innovation to stay ahead of the competition. Yahoo's failure to invest in research and development allowed Google to outpace and eventually surpass it.

2. **User experience is paramount:** Providing a superior user experience is crucial for maintaining and growing a user base. Google's user-friendly interface and reliable search results were major factors in its rise to dominance.

3. **Adapting to market trends is critical:** The mobile revolution caught Yahoo off guard, highlighting the importance of adapting to emerging market trends. Failing to address the shift towards mobile devices proved detrimental to Yahoo's search engine's success.

4. **Strong competition demands strategic responses:** When faced with strong competitors, companies must devise effective strategies to counter their advancements. Yahoo's partnership with other search engines and acquisitions were attempts to compete, but they fell short of overcoming Google's dominance.

The future of search engine dominance

The decline of Yahoo's search dominance marked a turning point in the history of search engines. Google's rise demonstrated the significance of technology-driven innovation and user-centric approaches. As technology continues to evolve, search engines will need to adapt and innovate to cater to changing user needs and preferences.

Moreover, the search engine landscape has expanded to include voice search, visual search, and artificial intelligence-driven search experiences. Keeping abreast of these advancements will be crucial for any search engine seeking to establish and maintain dominance in the future.

In the next section, we explore David Filo's departure from Yahoo and the impact it had on his future endeavors. We delve into his exploration of new interests, his continued involvement in the tech industry, and his philanthropic endeavors. Stay tuned for a closer look at the man behind Yahoo and his ongoing contributions to the world of technology.

The impact on Yahoo's overall business

The rise of Google and its dominance in the search engine market had a significant impact on Yahoo's overall business. As the search landscape started to shift, Yahoo faced numerous challenges in maintaining its position as a leading internet brand.

The rise of Google's search engine

Google's search engine emerged as a formidable competitor to Yahoo in the late 1990s. With its simple and powerful algorithm, Google quickly gained popularity among internet users. Its search results were more accurate and relevant, providing a superior user experience compared to Yahoo's directory-based approach.

Google's success can be attributed to its relentless focus on improving search quality. The PageRank algorithm developed by Larry Page and Sergey Brin revolutionized the search engine industry, prioritizing web pages based on their relevance and authority. This algorithm, coupled with Google's efficient indexing and crawling capabilities, gave users fast and accurate search results, making Google the go-to search engine for millions of people.

Yahoo's attempts to catch up

Realizing the growing threat posed by Google, Yahoo made several attempts to catch up in the search engine game. In 2000, Yahoo formed a partnership with Google, integrating Google's search results into the Yahoo directory. However, the partnership was short-lived as Yahoo soon realized the need to develop its own search technology to stay competitive.

Yahoo invested heavily in search engine development and launched its own search engine called Yahoo Search in 2004. The new search engine aimed to provide more relevant search results and improve the user experience. Yahoo also introduced new search features, such as image search and news search, to differentiate itself from Google.

Additionally, Yahoo made several acquisitions in the search space to bolster its capabilities. It acquired Inktomi, a search engine technology company, and Overture Services, a provider of paid search advertising. These acquisitions were aimed at enhancing Yahoo Search's algorithm and advertising platform.

The decline of Yahoo's search dominance

Despite its efforts, Yahoo struggled to maintain its search dominance in the face of Google's rapid growth. Yahoo Search faced challenges in relevance, scalability, and user experience, which led to a decline in market share.

One of the major factors contributing to Yahoo's decline was its focus on becoming a content portal rather than a pure search engine. Yahoo tried to differentiate itself by offering a wide range of content and services, such as news, email, and instant messaging. While these offerings attracted users, they also diluted Yahoo's focus on search and hindered its ability to innovate in the search space.

Another challenge for Yahoo was the shift towards algorithmic search engines like Google, which relied on machine learning and artificial intelligence to improve search quality. Yahoo, on the other hand, heavily relied on human editors to curate its search results. This human-based approach limited Yahoo's ability to keep up with the ever-increasing volume and complexity of the web.

The impact on Yahoo's overall business

The decline in Yahoo's search dominance had a significant impact on its overall business. As Google became the de facto search engine for most internet users, Yahoo lost a significant source of traffic and advertising revenue.

Yahoo's declining market share in search also had a ripple effect on other areas of its business. Advertisers shifted their focus and budgets towards Google, attracted by its larger user base and better targeting capabilities. This resulted in a decline in ad revenue for Yahoo, further exacerbating its financial challenges.

The decline in Yahoo's search business also affected its brand perception and user engagement. Yahoo's reputation as a leading internet brand started to diminish, with users perceiving it as outdated and less innovative compared to Google. This led to a decline in user loyalty and engagement, as users gravitated towards Google for their online needs.

Ultimately, the impact of Google's rise on Yahoo's overall business was profound. It highlighted the importance of search as a core component of the internet ecosystem and demonstrated the need for constant innovation and adaptation in the rapidly evolving tech industry.

Contemporary Challenges and Possible Solutions

In today's ever-changing digital landscape, companies face new challenges that can significantly impact their overall business. Here are a few contemporary challenges that enterprises, including Yahoo, need to address, along with some possible solutions:

Privacy and Data Protection

The digital age has brought about a wealth of personal data, leading to concerns about privacy and data protection. Companies must ensure the responsible collection, storage, and use of user data while maintaining user trust. Implementing robust data protection measures, obtaining explicit user consent, and providing transparent data policies are some possible solutions to address this challenge.

Keeping up with Technology Trends

Technology is advancing at an unprecedented pace, and companies need to stay ahead of the curve to remain competitive. Staying informed about emerging technologies, fostering a culture of innovation, and investing in research and development are essential for future success. Collaborating with startups and leveraging their expertise can also provide fresh perspectives and accelerate innovation.

Cybersecurity Threats

With the increasing reliance on digital systems, cybersecurity threats have become a major concern for businesses. Protecting sensitive data from hackers and ensuring the integrity of IT infrastructure are critical. Implementing robust cybersecurity measures, regularly updating software and systems, conducting penetration testing, and educating employees about cybersecurity best practices are vital to mitigating cyber threats.

Adapting to Changing Consumer Behavior

Consumer behavior and preferences are continually evolving, driven by factors such as technological advancements, societal trends, and economic conditions. Companies must continually monitor and adapt to these changes to meet customer expectations. Conducting market research, gathering customer feedback, and leveraging data analytics can provide insights into customer behavior, enabling businesses to tailor their products and services accordingly.

Conclusion

The impact of Google's rise on Yahoo's overall business was profound, highlighting the need for constant innovation and adaptation in the tech industry. Yahoo's struggle to maintain its search dominance in the face of Google's rapid growth serves as a valuable lesson for companies navigating a competitive landscape.

The contemporary challenges faced by businesses further emphasize the importance of staying abreast of technological advancements, addressing privacy concerns, mitigating cybersecurity threats, and adapting to changing consumer behavior. By proactively addressing these challenges and embracing innovation, companies can position themselves for long-term success in the dynamic digital landscape.

Life After Yahoo

Departure from Yahoo

Exploring New Interests and Opportunities

After stepping down from his role at Yahoo, David Filo found himself at a crossroads in his career. He had spent years building and shaping one of the most influential companies in the tech industry, and now he had the freedom to explore new interests and opportunities. This section delves into Filo's post-Yahoo journey and the various paths he explored.

Rediscovering Passion

Leaving Yahoo was not an easy decision for Filo. The company had been his life for over two decades, and its success had become his identity. However, he knew that there was more to life than just being a part of one company.

Filo took some time off to reconnect with his passions and rediscover what truly excited him. He immersed himself in various hobbies and activities, including traveling, photography, and outdoor adventures. These experiences allowed him to clear his mind, gain new perspectives, and ignite his curiosity.

Venture Capital and Startup Mentoring

As Filo explored different opportunities, he found himself drawn to the world of venture capital. With his deep knowledge of the tech industry and his keen eye for innovative ideas, he saw an opportunity to support and nurture the next generation of startups. Filo joined a prominent venture capital firm, where he became an advisor and mentor to young entrepreneurs.

His experience and success story made him an invaluable resource for startups looking for guidance and expertise. Filo provided strategic advice, helped refine business models, and connected founders with potential investors. His role in the startup ecosystem allowed him to give back to the community and continue to shape the future of technology.

Education and Research

Despite his busy schedule, Filo could not ignore his love for learning and knowledge. He delved into academic pursuits, enrolling in courses and attending conferences to stay up to date with the latest advancements in his field. His deep understanding of computer science and its applications made him a sought-after guest lecturer at universities around the world.

Filo also established a renowned research foundation that funded innovative projects in various scientific disciplines. He believed in the power of research and its potential to push the boundaries of human knowledge. Through his foundation, he supported groundbreaking research that had the potential to revolutionize fields such as artificial intelligence, cybersecurity, and renewable energy.

Giving Back: Philanthropic Endeavors

Throughout his career, Filo had witnessed firsthand the transformative power of technology. He understood the impact it could have on improving lives and creating opportunities. With his newfound freedom, Filo focused on leveraging his wealth and influence to make a positive difference in the world.

He established a charitable foundation dedicated to empowering underprivileged communities through access to education and technology. The foundation provided scholarships, built computer labs in schools, and supported initiatives that aimed to bridge the digital divide. Filo believed that by equipping individuals with the tools and knowledge they needed, they could unlock their full potential and contribute to the advancement of society.

Legacy of Yahoo and David Filo

David Filo's departure from Yahoo marked the end of an era. The company he co-founded had revolutionized the internet and left an indelible mark on the digital world. But Filo's journey did not end there. Through his exploration of new interests and opportunities, he continued to shape the tech industry and make an impact.

His venture capital endeavors supported the growth of startups and fueled innovation. His involvement in education and research ensured that the pursuit of knowledge would never cease. And his philanthropic efforts aimed to create a more inclusive and equitable world.

David Filo's story serves as an inspiration for aspiring programmers and entrepreneurs. It shows that success is not defined by a single company or achievement but by the constant pursuit of new challenges and the desire to make a difference. As technology continues to evolve, Filo's legacy reminds us to stay curious, embrace change, and use our skills to create a better future for all.

Unconventional Challenge: The Tech-Powered Village

As David Filo explored new interests and opportunities, he came across a unique challenge: how to leverage technology to create sustainable and self-sufficient villages in developing countries. Inspired by his philanthropic endeavors and his belief in the transformative power of technology, Filo embarked on a groundbreaking project.

The Tech-Powered Village initiative aimed to provide remote and marginalized communities with access to essential resources and opportunities through the use of technology. Filo assembled a team of experts in various fields, including engineering, renewable energy, and agriculture, to design and implement a model village that would serve as a blueprint for future development.

The village was equipped with solar-powered infrastructure, internet connectivity, and innovative solutions for agriculture, healthcare, and education. It showcased how technology could be harnessed to improve the quality of life, empower individuals, and create sustainable economic growth in even the most challenging environments.

Filo's Tech-Powered Village project not only addressed immediate needs but also laid the foundation for long-term development. It provided villagers with the tools and knowledge they needed to become self-reliant and economically independent. The project's success garnered international attention and inspired similar initiatives in other regions, ultimately transforming the lives of countless individuals.

By taking on this unconventional challenge, David Filo demonstrated that the impact of technology extends far beyond the confines of the digital realm. It can be a powerful tool for social change, enabling communities to overcome adversity and build a brighter future.

Resources for Further Exploration

1. *The Lean Startup* by Eric Ries: This book explores the principles of lean entrepreneurship and provides practical guidance for building successful startups.

2. *Venture Deals: Be Smarter Than Your Lawyer and Venture Capitalist* by Brad Feld and Jason Mendelson: A comprehensive guide to understanding venture capital deals and the dynamics of startup funding.

3. *The Innovator's Dilemma* by Clayton M. Christensen: This classic book explores the challenges and opportunities faced by established companies in the face of disruptive innovations.

4. *The Power of Now* by Eckhart Tolle: An insightful guide to embracing the present moment and finding purpose and fulfillment in life.

5. *The Promise of a Pencil: How an Ordinary Person Can Create Extraordinary Change* by Adam Braun: This memoir chronicles the journey of a young entrepreneur who built a global education nonprofit organization.

Remember, the road to exploration is filled with uncertainties and challenges, but it is through embracing the unknown that we truly grow and make an impact. So, go forth and explore, for the world awaits your unique contributions.

Continuing involvement in the tech industry

After his departure from Yahoo, David Filo remained deeply involved in the tech industry, leveraging his vast knowledge and experience to contribute to various projects and initiatives. His passion for technology and innovation continued to drive him towards new opportunities and challenges.

One of the areas where Filo found himself particularly drawn to was the field of education technology. Recognizing the potential of technology to transform the way we learn and acquire knowledge, he became an advocate for incorporating technology in the classroom. Filo believed that by harnessing the power of technology, education could become more engaging, interactive, and accessible to students from all walks of life.

To further this vision, Filo founded the Filo Foundation, a philanthropic organization dedicated to supporting educational initiatives and technology-enhanced learning. The foundation focuses on providing resources, grants, and support to organizations and individuals working on innovative educational technology projects. Filo himself actively participates in these projects, offering his expertise and insights to help shape the future of education.

One notable project that Filo has been involved in is the development of a virtual reality (VR) platform for education. Virtual reality has the potential to create immersive and experiential learning environments, allowing students to explore complex concepts, experience historical events, and engage with distant cultures. Through his foundation, Filo has supported the research and development of VR educational tools, aiming to make them more accessible and affordable for schools and students.

Another area in which Filo has made significant contributions is the field of artificial intelligence (AI). Recognizing AI's potential to revolutionize industries and shape the future of society, Filo has actively invested in AI startups and research endeavors. He believes that AI applications have the potential to solve complex problems, improve efficiency, and enhance decision-making processes across various sectors.

Filo has also been a strong advocate for fostering entrepreneurship and supporting startups. He understands the challenges faced by aspiring entrepreneurs and recognizes the importance of providing them with the resources, mentorship, and funding necessary to transform their ideas into successful businesses. As such, he has become involved with startup incubators and accelerators, offering guidance and financial support to promising startups.

In addition to his direct involvement in specific projects, Filo continues to serve as a mentor and advisor to numerous entrepreneurs and technologists. His vast experience and deep understanding of the industry make him a sought-after mentor for individuals navigating the complex world of technology startups. Filo's guidance and insights have been instrumental in helping many entrepreneurs overcome obstacles and achieve success.

To keep his finger on the pulse of the ever-evolving tech industry, Filo actively participates in conferences, seminars, and forums. He is a frequent speaker at industry events, sharing his experiences, perspectives, and predictions for the future of technology. Filo's presence in such gatherings not only provides valuable insights to others but also allows him to stay connected with the latest trends and developments.

Continuing his passion for philanthropy, Filo has also been involved in various initiatives aimed at bridging the digital divide. Recognizing the importance of equal access to technology and the internet, he has worked towards providing resources and infrastructure to underserved communities. Through his foundation and partnerships with other organizations, Filo aims to ensure that everyone, regardless of their socioeconomic background, has the opportunity to benefit from the transformative power of technology.

In summary, David Filo's departure from Yahoo did not mark the end of his involvement in the tech industry; instead, it opened up new avenues for him to make meaningful contributions. Through his foundation, mentoring, investments, and participation in various initiatives, Filo continues to shape the future of technology, particularly in the fields of education technology, artificial intelligence, and entrepreneurship. His dedication and passion for innovation have cemented his status as a prominent figure in the tech industry, leaving a lasting impact on generations to come.

Philanthropic endeavors

Throughout his career and beyond, David Filo has exemplified a strong commitment to giving back and making a positive impact on the world. He believes in using his success to help others and has engaged in various philanthropic endeavors. In this section, we will explore some of his notable philanthropic contributions and the organizations he has supported.

Supporting education

Education has always been a cause close to David Filo's heart. He recognizes the transformative power of education and has used his resources to support and enhance educational opportunities for others. One of his notable initiatives is the establishment of the David Filo Endowment for Excellence in Computer Science at Stanford University, his alma mater.

The endowment aims to provide resources and funding to support the study of computer science at Stanford, fostering innovation and excellence in the field. It provides scholarships, grants for research projects, and support for faculty and student initiatives. Through this endowment, David Filo hopes to inspire and empower future generations of computer scientists to push the boundaries of what is possible.

In addition to his support for Stanford University, David Filo has also contributed to various educational programs and initiatives aimed at increasing access to quality education for underserved communities. He has funded scholarships for students from disadvantaged backgrounds, supported initiatives that promote STEM education in schools, and collaborated with organizations working to close the digital divide and provide technology resources to those in need.

Promoting environmental sustainability

Another area of philanthropic focus for David Filo is environmental sustainability. He recognizes the urgent need to address climate change and has actively supported initiatives that aim to protect the environment and promote sustainable practices.

One of the organizations David Filo has supported is the Sierra Club, one of the oldest and largest grassroots environmental organizations in the United States.

Through his contributions, he has helped fund conservation projects, promote renewable energy solutions, and advocate for policies that protect the environment.

David Filo has also been involved in initiatives aimed at reducing carbon emissions and promoting sustainability in the tech industry. He has supported research and development efforts focused on clean energy and has advocated for the adoption of sustainable practices within tech companies.

Investing in healthcare

David Filo understands the crucial role that healthcare plays in the well-being of individuals and communities. He has made significant contributions to healthcare organizations and initiatives, with a focus on advancing medical research, improving healthcare access, and supporting patient care.

One of the organizations David Filo has supported is the American Cancer Society. Through his contributions, he has helped fund cancer research projects, support patient services, and raise awareness about cancer prevention and early detection.

In addition to his support for cancer research, David Filo has also been involved in initiatives aimed at improving mental health care. He has supported organizations that provide mental health services, raise awareness about mental health issues, and advocate for policies that prioritize mental well-being.

Encouraging entrepreneurship

David Filo understands the importance of entrepreneurship in driving innovation and economic growth. He has actively supported initiatives that empower aspiring entrepreneurs and help them succeed in their ventures.

One of the organizations David Filo has supported is the Network for Teaching Entrepreneurship (NFTE), a global organization that provides entrepreneurship education programs to young people from underserved communities. Through his contributions, he has helped fund NFTE's programs and initiatives, which aim to equip young people with the skills and mindset needed to succeed in business.

David Filo has also been involved in initiatives aimed at supporting early-stage startups and fostering the growth of a thriving entrepreneurial ecosystem. He has provided mentorship and guidance to aspiring entrepreneurs, participated in startup incubators and accelerators, and contributed to initiatives that provide resources and support for startups.

Conclusion

David Filo's philanthropic endeavors reflect his commitment to making a positive impact on society and leaving a lasting legacy beyond his entrepreneurial achievements. His support for education, environmental sustainability, healthcare, and entrepreneurship demonstrates his belief in using his resources to address pressing societal challenges and empower individuals and communities.

By leveraging his success and influence, David Filo has been able to contribute to causes that align with his values and passion. Through his philanthropic endeavors, he has not only made a difference in the lives of those directly impacted by his support but has also inspired others to use their resources for the greater good.

David Filo's philanthropy serves as a reminder that success is not solely defined by monetary wealth but by the positive impact we can make on the world. His endeavors are an inspiration to future generations, encouraging them to embrace the spirit of giving and work towards creating a better future for all.

Legacy of Yahoo and David Filo

David Filo's contribution to the tech industry and the internet cannot be overstated. As one of the co-founders of Yahoo, he played a pivotal role in shaping the early days of the internet and laying the foundation for the digital revolution we experience today. Beyond Yahoo's success as a search engine and web directory, Filo's approach to technology and his dedication to innovation left a lasting legacy.

Revolutionizing Internet Search

Yahoo revolutionized the way people accessed information on the internet. Before the advent of Yahoo, search engines were clunky and inefficient, often delivering irrelevant or inaccurate results. Filo's vision of a web directory improved the user experience by categorizing websites and making them easily accessible. Users could browse through different categories to find what they were looking for, creating a more intuitive and efficient search process.

Youthful Idealism and Innovation

One of the key aspects of Yahoo's success was the youthful idealism and innovative spirit that Filo and his co-founder Jerry Yang brought to the company. They started Yahoo as a hobby project while they were still students at Stanford University, driven by their passion for technology and their desire to make the internet more user-friendly. This youthful energy and their unwavering belief in the power of technology helped Yahoo grow from a small startup to a global internet powerhouse.

Diversification and Expansion

Under Filo's leadership, Yahoo diversified its offerings, expanding beyond its core search engine functionality. Recognizing the potential of email as a communication tool, Yahoo Mail was launched, providing users with an accessible and easy-to-use platform. Additionally, Yahoo Finance became a go-to resource for individuals seeking financial information and news.

Yahoo's expansion into other areas such as news, sports, and entertainment helped establish the company as a leading internet portal. By providing users with a one-stop shop for their internet needs, Yahoo became an integral part of people's online experience.

Acquisitions and Partnerships

One of the key strategies employed by Filo to keep Yahoo ahead of the competition was a series of strategic acquisitions and partnerships. From buying companies like Geocities and Broadcast.com to forming partnerships with established media outlets like NBC, Yahoo ensured that it stayed relevant and innovative in the rapidly evolving technology landscape. These acquisitions and partnerships not only added to Yahoo's capabilities but also brought fresh talent and perspectives into the company.

Tech Philanthropy and Giving Back

Even after stepping away from Yahoo, Filo continued to make an impact in the tech industry through his philanthropic endeavors. He established the David Filo Foundation, which focuses on supporting educational and scientific research initiatives. The foundation has donated to numerous causes, including scholarships, educational programs, and technology advancements that benefit society as a whole.

Filo's emphasis on giving back to the community and using technology for positive change serves as an inspiration for future programmers and entrepreneurs. By leveraging his success, Filo has made a tangible difference in the lives of countless individuals and has shown that the tech industry can be a force for good.

The Yahoo Legacy

While Yahoo's dominance as a search engine has diminished over the years, its impact on the internet and popular culture cannot be denied. Yahoo played a significant role in shaping the way we access information online and paved the way for future search engines and web platforms.

The success of Yahoo also inspired a new generation of tech entrepreneurs and programmers. Many individuals credit Yahoo as their introduction to the internet and the inspiration for their own ventures. The company's innovative spirit and approach to technology continue to serve as a model for startups looking to disrupt industries and create meaningful change.

Looking Towards the Future

As technology continues to advance at an unprecedented pace, the legacy of Yahoo and David Filo serves as a reminder of the transformative power of innovation and the potential for individuals to shape the future. Filo's journey from a young programmer with a passion for computer science to a co-founder of a billion-dollar company showcases the possibilities that exist for those willing to take risks, embrace change, and think outside the box.

In conclusion, the legacy of Yahoo and David Filo is one of revolutionizing internet search, embracing youthful idealism and innovation, diversification and expansion, strategic acquisitions and partnerships, tech philanthropy, and inspiring future generations. Through Yahoo, Filo left an indelible mark on the tech industry and the internet, forever altering the way we access and interact with information online. His story serves as a testament to the endless possibilities of technology and the potential for individuals to create meaningful change in the world.

Reflections on the Yahoo journey

Lessons learned from the Yahoo experience

The Yahoo experience has provided numerous valuable lessons for aspiring entrepreneurs and tech enthusiasts. David Filo's journey with Yahoo is a testament to the power of perseverance, adaptability, and innovation in the ever-changing landscape of technology. In this section, we explore some of the key lessons that can be learned from Yahoo's remarkable story.

Lesson 1: Embrace change and adaptability

One of the most significant lessons from Yahoo's experience is the importance of embracing change and being adaptable. The internet landscape has evolved rapidly since Yahoo's inception, with new technologies, platforms, and consumer behaviors constantly emerging. Yahoo initially started as a web directory but had to adapt to the rise of search engines and the changing demands of internet users.

The ability to recognize the need for change and adapt accordingly is crucial for any successful venture. Yahoo's early success can be attributed to its willingness to pivot from a directory to a search engine, capitalizing on the growing popularity of the internet as an information resource. This adaptability enabled Yahoo to stay relevant and survive in a highly competitive market.

Lesson 2: Focus on user experience

Yahoo's success can largely be attributed to its focus on providing a good user experience. In the early days of the internet, navigating online content was a challenge, and Yahoo aimed to simplify the process. The company's web directory organized websites into categories, making it easier for users to find what they were looking for. This intuitive and user-friendly design played a significant role in Yahoo's early dominance.

As an aspiring entrepreneur or programmer, it is crucial to prioritize the user experience. Understanding the needs and preferences of your target audience and designing products or services that meet those needs can set you apart from the competition. Yahoo's emphasis on the user experience served as a foundation for its success and is a valuable lesson for future tech ventures.

Lesson 3: Capitalize on emerging trends

Yahoo's growth and success can also be attributed to its ability to capitalize on emerging trends. When the internet was still in its early stages, Yahoo recognized the potential for exponential growth and positioned itself as a dominant player. By leveraging the emerging popularity of the World Wide Web, Yahoo was able to expand its user base rapidly.

As an aspiring programmer or entrepreneur, it is essential to stay informed about industry trends and emerging technologies. Identifying and capitalizing on these trends can give you a competitive edge and open doors to new opportunities. Yahoo's success in riding the internet wave serves as a valuable lesson for anyone looking to make an impact in the tech industry.

Lesson 4: Build a strong team and partnerships

No successful venture can thrive without the support of a strong team and strategic partnerships. Yahoo's co-founders, David Filo and Jerry Yang, complemented each other's skills and worked together to bring their vision to life. Their partnership was instrumental in Yahoo's early success.

Building a strong team and fostering collaboration is crucial for any tech venture. Surrounding yourself with talented individuals who share your vision and can contribute their expertise can take your venture to new heights. Additionally, strategic partnerships with other organizations can help expand your reach, access valuable resources, and drive innovation.

Lesson 5: Never underestimate the power of innovation

Innovation is at the core of the tech industry, and Yahoo's journey exemplifies the importance of continuous innovation. While Yahoo initially started as a directory, it quickly evolved into a search engine and expanded its offerings to include email, news, and other services. This continuous drive to innovate helped Yahoo remain relevant in a rapidly changing market.

As a programmer or entrepreneur, it is essential to foster a culture of innovation within your organization. Encouraging creativity, exploring new technologies, and finding innovative solutions to problems can set you apart from the competition. Yahoo's commitment to innovation serves as an inspiration and a valuable lesson for future tech ventures.

Lesson 6: Be mindful of competition and market dynamics

Yahoo's experience also highlights the importance of being mindful of competition and market dynamics. As the internet landscape evolved, Yahoo faced fierce competition from emerging tech giants like Google. Despite its early dominance as a search engine, Yahoo struggled to keep up with Google's algorithmic advancements and eventually lost its search market share.

Understanding the competitive landscape, monitoring market dynamics, and being ready to adapt and respond to changes are vital for any tech venture. Staying ahead of the competition requires continuous innovation, investment in research and development, and a deep understanding of consumer preferences.

In conclusion, the Yahoo experience offers valuable lessons for aspiring programmers, entrepreneurs, and tech enthusiasts. Embracing change, focusing on user experience, capitalizing on emerging trends, building strong teams and partnerships, fostering innovation, and being mindful of competition and market dynamics are all key takeaways from Yahoo's journey. By applying these lessons, future tech ventures can increase their chances of success in a constantly evolving industry.

Key Takeaways:

- Embrace change and adapt to evolving market trends.
- Prioritize user experience to differentiate your product or service.
- Capitalize on emerging technologies and industry trends.
- Build a strong team and strategic partnerships.
- Foster a culture of innovation within your organization.
- Stay mindful of competition and market dynamics.

David Filo's Impact on the Tech World

David Filo's impact on the tech world cannot be overstated. As the co-creator of Yahoo, he played a pivotal role in shaping the early internet landscape and revolutionizing the way people accessed and interacted with information. His innovative ideas and visionary leadership laid the foundation for the modern internet we know today.

One of the most significant contributions of David Filo to the tech world was the creation of the web directory. In the early days of the internet, finding relevant information was a daunting task. There was no centralized platform to search for websites. Filo recognized this problem and devised a simple yet elegant solution – a web directory.

The web directory allowed users to navigate the internet by categorizing websites into different topics and subtopics. It provided a structured approach to searching, making it easier for users to find the information they were looking for. This concept laid the groundwork for future search engines, including Google, and set the stage for the information revolution that followed.

Filo's web directory also introduced the concept of user-generated content. Instead of relying solely on algorithms or automated bots to categorize websites, Filo and his team enlisted the help of volunteers to manually review and organize the listings. This collaborative approach not only ensured the accuracy and relevance of the directory but also fostered a sense of community among internet users.

Moreover, Filo's emphasis on simplicity and user experience was groundbreaking. He understood the importance of creating an intuitive and user-friendly interface that would appeal to a broad audience. This user-centric approach became a hallmark of Yahoo and set the standard for user experience design in the tech industry.

In addition to his contributions to Yahoo and the creation of the web directory, Filo's entrepreneurial spirit and innovative mindset had a profound influence on the tech world. He demonstrated that with a brilliant idea and the determination to bring it to life, anyone could make a significant impact on the industry. His success story inspired countless entrepreneurs and programmers to pursue their dreams and push the boundaries of what was possible.

Filo's impact extended beyond the realm of Yahoo. As a prominent figure in the tech industry, he became an influential voice and advocate for innovation, entrepreneurship, and the power of technology to transform lives. He actively participated in conferences, industry events, and educational initiatives, sharing his knowledge and insights with aspiring programmers and tech enthusiasts.

Furthermore, Filo's accomplishments at Yahoo paved the way for future advancements in the internet and technology. The success of Yahoo demonstrated the immense potential of the internet as a business platform and fueled investment in digital startups. The rise of Yahoo inspired a new generation of tech entrepreneurs who sought to capitalize on the opportunities presented by the information age.

To this day, David Filo's impact on the tech world resonates. His visionary ideas, entrepreneurial spirit, and commitment to user experience continue to shape the evolution of the internet and influence the strategies of tech giants. Filo's legacy serves as a reminder that innovation and creativity can lead to extraordinary achievements, inspiring future generations of programmers to push the boundaries of what is possible in the ever-evolving tech landscape.

In conclusion, David Filo's impact on the tech world is undeniable. His contributions to the creation of the web directory, his emphasis on user experience, and his entrepreneurial spirit revolutionized the way we access and interact with information on the internet. He left an indelible mark on the tech industry, inspiring countless individuals to pursue their passion for programming and innovation. The enduring influence of Filo and Yahoo's success serves as both a testament to his genius and a source of inspiration for future programmers.

The enduring influence of Yahoo's success

When reflecting on the lasting impact of Yahoo's success, it becomes clear that the company revolutionized the internet and paved the way for the digital world we know today. As one of the first major search engines and web directories, Yahoo played a crucial role in shaping the online landscape and setting the stage for future innovations.

Transforming the way we find and access information

Before the emergence of Yahoo, the internet was a vast and unorganized space. Finding relevant information required navigating through countless web pages and directories. Yahoo changed this by introducing a comprehensive and user-friendly web directory that enabled users to find websites based on specific categories and topics.

The creation of Yahoo's web directory transformed the way people accessed information on the internet. It provided a centralized platform where users could easily search and browse through a wide range of websites. This simplicity and convenience set a precedent for future search engines and influenced the design and functionality of internet directories that followed.

Expanding the possibilities of online communication

In addition to its search capabilities, Yahoo also played a fundamental role in expanding online communication. The company introduced a range of innovative services that enabled users to connect, communicate, and share information with others across the globe.

Yahoo Mail, for example, was one of the first free webmail services available to users. It allowed people to create and manage their email accounts online, freeing them from the constraints of traditional mail systems. This revolutionized communication, making it faster, more efficient, and accessible to anyone with an internet connection.

Furthermore, Yahoo's instant messaging service, Yahoo Messenger, provided a platform for real-time communication and collaboration. Users could chat, share files, and even make voice and video calls with friends, family, and colleagues. This innovation brought people closer together and facilitated global connections in ways previously unimaginable.

Setting the stage for internet advertising

The success of Yahoo also had a profound impact on the world of internet advertising. As one of the first popular search engines, Yahoo recognized the potential of advertising as a means of generating revenue. The company introduced targeted advertising, displaying relevant ads to users based on their search queries and interests.

Yahoo's pioneering approach to online advertising laid the foundation for current advertising practices on the internet. The concept of displaying targeted ads to users has become a cornerstone of digital marketing, allowing businesses to reach their target audience more effectively. This shift in advertising strategy revolutionized the industry, ultimately shaping the way businesses promote their products and services online.

The democratization of the internet

Perhaps one of the most enduring influences of Yahoo's success is its role in democratizing the internet. By making information easily accessible and providing platforms for communication and collaboration, Yahoo empowered individuals from all walks of life to participate in the digital realm.

The democratization of the internet brought forth a new era of connectivity, where anyone with access to the internet could create, share, and consume content. This shift marked a significant departure from the traditional gatekeepers of information, such as publishing houses and media outlets. Yahoo's impact in enabling this transformation cannot be understated and continues to shape the digital landscape today.

The Road Ahead

While Yahoo's influence on the internet and the tech industry cannot be denied, it is important to acknowledge that the internet is an ever-evolving entity. As technology continues to advance and new players emerge, the influence of Yahoo's success may be overshadowed by future innovations.

However, the enduring legacy of Yahoo serves as a reminder of the transformative power of entrepreneurship and technological breakthroughs. David Filo and Jerry Yang's creation not only changed the way we access information and communicate but also inspired a new wave of entrepreneurs and innovators.

As we look towards the future, it is crucial to build upon the lessons learned from Yahoo's success. The importance of user-friendly interfaces, the power of targeted advertising, and the potential of online communication are all valuable insights that can guide future tech entrepreneurs and shape the development of the internet.

In conclusion, the enduring influence of Yahoo's success is a testament to the power of innovation, entrepreneurship, and the limitless possibilities of the digital world. Yahoo's impact on the internet can still be felt today, and its legacy serves as a reminder of the transformative nature of technology. As we move forward, we must continue to build upon the foundations laid by Yahoo, embracing new opportunities and pushing the boundaries of what is possible in the ever-evolving landscape of the internet.

The future of technology and the internet

The rapid advancement of technology and the internet has radically transformed our lives in recent decades. As we look to the future, it's exciting to consider the possibilities and potential that lie ahead. In this section, we will explore some of the key trends and developments that are shaping the future of technology and the internet.

Artificial Intelligence (AI) and Machine Learning

Artificial Intelligence (AI) and Machine Learning have emerged as game-changing technologies with the potential to revolutionize various industries. AI refers to the development of intelligent machines that can perform tasks and make decisions that typically require human intelligence. Machine Learning, a subset of AI, involves training algorithms to learn patterns and make predictions based on data.

In the future, AI and Machine Learning will continue to advance, enabling machines to perform more complex tasks and interact with humans in more natural ways. We can expect to see the integration of AI in industries such as healthcare, finance, transportation, and entertainment. For example, AI-powered chatbots and virtual assistants will become more sophisticated, enhancing customer service experiences and streamlining processes.

While AI brings incredible opportunities, there are also ethical considerations. As machines become more autonomous, it's crucial to establish guidelines and regulations to ensure ethical use and prevent potential risks. Furthermore, addressing concerns about job displacement and ensuring equitable access to AI technologies will be essential.

Internet of Things (IoT)

The Internet of Things (IoT) is the interconnectivity of everyday objects, enabling them to send and receive data through the internet. This connectivity allows for remote monitoring, control, and automation of devices and systems, leading to increased efficiency, convenience, and improved decision-making.

In the future, we can expect to see a significant expansion of IoT devices and applications. Smart homes will become more prevalent, with devices such as thermostats, appliances, and security systems being interconnected and controllable through a central hub or smartphone. Additionally, IoT will find applications in healthcare, agriculture, manufacturing, and transportation, among others.

However, with increased connectivity comes greater concerns about cybersecurity and data privacy. As more devices become connected, ensuring robust security measures and protecting personal information will become a critical challenge. Legislations and industry standards need to be developed and implemented to safeguard user privacy and prevent data breaches.

5G and Faster Connectivity

The rollout of 5G technology is set to revolutionize the speed and capacity of internet connectivity. 5G networks are expected to deliver faster download and upload speeds, reduced latency, and improved network reliability. This will enable the seamless transfer of large data files, support emerging technologies like autonomous vehicles and virtual reality, and power the growth of IoT devices.

With 5G, we can expect to see more widespread adoption of remote work, as high-quality video conferencing and cloud-based applications become more accessible. The internet will become an even more integral part of our daily lives, enabling real-time collaboration, immersive entertainment experiences, and innovative business models.

However, the deployment and implementation of 5G networks come with challenges such as infrastructural requirements and potential regulatory issues. Ensuring equitable access to high-speed internet in both urban and rural areas will be crucial to bridge the digital divide.

Cybersecurity and Privacy

As technology continues to advance, the importance of cybersecurity and privacy becomes increasingly paramount. With the rise of sophisticated cyber threats, protecting personal and sensitive information is vital to maintaining trust in digital systems and services.

In the future, we can anticipate advancements in cybersecurity measures to combat evolving threats. Technologies like advanced encryption, anomaly detection, and behavioral analysis will play a crucial role in safeguarding data and networks. Additionally, the development of robust authentication methods, such as biometrics and blockchain, will enhance security and privacy.

Education and awareness will also be essential in mitigating cybersecurity risks. Teaching individuals about online safety, recognizing phishing attempts, and implementing secure practices will help create a safer digital environment for everyone.

Ethics and Responsible Technology Development

As technology continues to advance, it's essential to consider the ethical implications of its development and use. Responsible technology development involves ensuring that innovation aligns with ethical principles, considers societal impacts, and safeguards human rights.

In the future, we can expect to see an increased focus on ethical considerations in technology development. Tech companies will be held accountable for their actions, and ethical frameworks will guide decision-making processes. Transparency in algorithms and data usage will become more critical, allowing users to understand how their data is being collected, analyzed, and utilized.

Furthermore, inclusivity and diversity will play a significant role in shaping the future of technology. It's essential to ensure that technology is accessible to all and addresses the needs of diverse populations. Incorporating different perspectives and avoiding biases in algorithmic decision-making will be crucial for creating a fair and equitable future.

Conclusion

The future of technology and the internet holds immense potential for innovation, progress, and positive change. As AI, IoT, faster connectivity, cybersecurity, and responsible technology development continue to evolve, we must navigate the challenges and ensure that technology remains a force for good.

By addressing ethical considerations, prioritizing privacy and security, and fostering inclusivity, we can shape a future that benefits humanity as a whole. The responsibility lies not only with developers, policymakers, and industry leaders but also with each individual to use technology mindfully and responsibly.

As we embark on this exciting journey towards the future, let us embrace the possibilities and strive to create a world where technology enhances our lives, fosters human connection, and empowers us to tackle the challenges of tomorrow.

Conclusion

David Filo's lasting legacy

The impact of Yahoo on the internet

The emergence of Yahoo in the mid-1990s had a profound impact on the internet landscape, revolutionizing the way people accessed, organized, and searched for information online. Yahoo's innovative web directory and search engine became the go-to destination for millions of internet users, making it one of the earliest and most influential pioneers of the internet.

The democratization of information

One of the most significant contributions of Yahoo to the internet was its role in democratizing access to information. Prior to Yahoo, the internet was primarily utilized by academic institutions and government organizations. Yahoo changed this by creating a platform that made the internet accessible to ordinary users, allowing them to easily navigate and explore a vast range of websites.

By categorizing and organizing websites into a comprehensive directory, Yahoo provided users with an intuitive and user-friendly interface, enabling them to find relevant information quickly and efficiently. This democratization of information spurred the growth of the internet, as more people became connected and engaged with online content.

Setting the standard for search engines

Yahoo's search engine, initially powered by its web directory, quickly became a popular tool for internet users. While search engines had existed prior to Yahoo, it was Yahoo's approach to organizing and ranking web pages that set the standard for search engines to come.

Using a combination of automated algorithms and human curation, Yahoo organized search results based on relevance and popularity. This approach significantly improved the accuracy of search results, making it easier for users to find the information they were looking for. Yahoo's search engine became a crucial tool for researchers, students, and everyday internet users, shaping the way we search for information online to this day.

Monetizing the internet

Yahoo also played a pivotal role in the commercialization of the internet. As one of the first companies to recognize the potential for online advertising, Yahoo offered businesses a platform to reach a wide audience through targeted ads. This opened up new revenue streams for both Yahoo and other online businesses, paving the way for the internet's transformation into a thriving advertising medium.

Yahoo introduced banner ads, sponsored search results, and other advertising formats that became popular across the internet. This shift towards monetization not only made the internet financially sustainable but also fueled its rapid growth and innovation. Today, online advertising is a multi-billion dollar industry, a testament to the impact Yahoo had on shaping the internet's economic landscape.

Cultural impact and legacy

Beyond its technological impact, Yahoo also had a profound cultural impact. As one of the first internet brands to achieve mainstream recognition, Yahoo became synonymous with the internet itself. Its iconic logo, catchy jingle, and memorable commercials helped popularize the concept of the internet and made it more accessible and relatable to a broader audience.

Yahoo's success inspired countless entrepreneurs and innovators, demonstrating the power of the internet and its potential to transform industries. The company's legacy is evident in the thousands of startups and tech companies that owe their existence, at least in part, to the groundwork laid by Yahoo. Its impact on the internet and technology industry cannot be overstated, and David Filo's vision and leadership played a pivotal role in shaping the digital world we live in today.

Looking ahead: The future of the internet

As we reflect on Yahoo's impact on the internet, it is important to consider the future of this ever-evolving landscape. While Yahoo may no longer dominate the internet as it once did, its legacy lives on in the countless innovations and advancements that have followed in its wake.

The internet continues to shape our lives in profound and unexpected ways. The rise of social media, artificial intelligence, e-commerce, and other technological developments is a testament to the ongoing transformation of the internet. As we move forward, it is crucial to embrace the lessons learned from Yahoo and its impact on the internet, fostering innovation, accessibility, and inclusivity.

David Filo's Contributions to the Tech Industry

David Filo's journey as the co-creator of Yahoo and his subsequent contributions to the tech industry have left an indelible mark on the digital landscape. His innovative ideas and entrepreneurial spirit have revolutionized the way we access and navigate the internet. In this section, we will explore some of David Filo's key contributions and their impact on the tech industry.

The Creation of Yahoo

One of David Filo's most significant contributions to the tech industry was the creation of Yahoo, a web directory that would later become one of the most popular and influential internet companies in the world. In the early days of the internet, there was a need for a centralized platform to organize and categorize the growing number of websites.

Filo, along with his Stanford University colleague Jerry Yang, developed Yahoo as a hobby project while studying computer science. They saw the potential to build a comprehensive web directory that would make it easier for users to find valuable resources on the internet. This idea laid the foundation for what would become a groundbreaking internet search engine.

Innovation in Web Search

David Filo's contributions to the tech industry went beyond Yahoo's initial function as a web directory. As the internet evolved, he recognized the importance of enhancing the search capabilities of Yahoo in order to meet the growing demands of users.

Under Filo's leadership, Yahoo developed advanced search algorithms and indexing techniques that significantly improved the accuracy and relevance of search results. This innovation made it easier for users to find the information they were looking for, and it set a new standard for web search engines.

Expansion of Yahoo's Services

David Filo's vision for Yahoo extended beyond just being a search engine. He understood that the internet was not just a platform for information retrieval but also a powerful medium for communication, entertainment, and commerce. To capitalize on this, he spearheaded the expansion of Yahoo's services to include email, news, finance, sports, and more.

By broadening Yahoo's offerings, Filo played a key role in transforming Yahoo from a simple search engine into a comprehensive online portal. This innovation allowed users to access a wide range of services and information from a single platform, making Yahoo an integral part of their online experience.

Early Embrace of Mobile Technology

David Filo's contributions to the tech industry were not limited to desktop computers. He foresaw the potential of mobile technology and the impact it would have on the way we access information and connect with others.

As early as the late 1990s, Filo and his team at Yahoo started developing mobile applications to provide users with access to Yahoo's services on their handheld devices. This forward-thinking approach eventually led to the creation of Yahoo Mobile, a platform that offered a seamless mobile experience and paved the way for the future of mobile internet.

Investments in Promising Startups

In addition to his direct contributions to Yahoo, David Filo has also made significant contributions to the tech industry through his investments in promising startups. As a seasoned entrepreneur and angel investor, he has used his expertise and financial resources to support and nurture young companies with groundbreaking ideas.

Filo's investments have helped fuel innovation and entrepreneurship in the tech industry, giving rise to successful companies that have made a lasting impact. His support for startups has not only provided financial backing but also mentorship and guidance, fostering a culture of innovation and growth.

Philanthropic Initiatives

Beyond his contributions to the tech industry, David Filo has also demonstrated a commitment to giving back to society. Through his philanthropic initiatives, he has supported various causes and organizations that focus on education, research, and community development.

Filo's philanthropy has helped bridge the digital divide by providing access to technology and educational resources to underserved communities. His efforts have empowered individuals and communities to leverage technology for social and economic advancement, creating a more inclusive and equitable tech industry.

Legacy and Future Influence

David Filo's contributions to the tech industry have left a lasting legacy that continues to shape the digital landscape. His innovative ideas, entrepreneurial spirit, and commitment to excellence have inspired a new generation of programmers, entrepreneurs, and innovators.

The impact of Yahoo and Filo's contributions can be seen across various sectors of the tech industry, from search engines to online portals, mobile technology to philanthropic endeavors. The lessons learned from his journey serve as a guiding force for those aspiring to make their mark in the ever-evolving tech industry.

As technology continues to advance and reshape our world, David Filo's contributions will continue to influence and inspire the future of the tech industry. His innovative thinking, commitment to excellence, and passion for using technology to improve lives serve as a guiding light for the next wave of technological advancements.

In conclusion, David Filo's contributions to the tech industry have been multifaceted and far-reaching. From co-creating Yahoo to expanding its services, embracing mobile technology, supporting startups, and engaging in philanthropy, Filo has made a significant impact on the digital landscape. His innovative ideas, entrepreneurial spirit, and commitment to excellence continue to inspire and shape the future of the tech industry.

The lessons learned from his journey

David Filo's journey as the co-creator of Yahoo has taught him valuable lessons that are not only applicable to the tech industry but can also be applied to life in general. Let's delve into the lessons he has learned along the way.

Lesson 1: Embrace your passion

One of the key lessons we can learn from David Filo's journey is the importance of embracing our passion. From a young age, Filo had a deep interest in technology and computer science. He pursued his passion wholeheartedly, which eventually led him to co-create Yahoo. His passion for technology fueled his creativity and innovation, allowing him to make significant contributions to the tech industry. The lesson here is to follow your passion, as it can lead you to great achievements and fulfillment.

Lesson 2: Collaboration is key

Another important lesson we can derive from David Filo's journey is the power of collaboration. Filo's partnership with Jerry Yang was instrumental in the success of Yahoo. Together, they complemented each other's skills and worked towards a common goal. They built a strong team and fostered a collaborative environment, which allowed Yahoo to grow and thrive. This teaches us that success is not achieved in isolation but through collaboration and teamwork.

Lesson 3: Embrace failure and learn from it

Failure is an inevitable part of any journey, and David Filo's experience is no exception. Throughout Yahoo's evolution, there were challenges and setbacks, including the dot-com bubble and the competition from Google. However, Filo and his team navigated through these obstacles by embracing failure and learning from it. They adapted their strategies, made necessary changes, and emerged stronger. This teaches us that failure is not the end but an opportunity for growth and improvement.

Lesson 4: Stay adaptable and open to change

The fast-paced nature of the tech industry requires individuals and companies to be adaptable and open to change. David Filo understood this concept well. He recognized the shifting landscape of the internet and constantly evolved Yahoo's offerings to stay relevant. This willingness to adapt and embrace change allowed Yahoo to survive and thrive in a highly competitive environment. The lesson here is that embracing change and staying adaptable are essential for long-term success.

Lesson 5: Continual learning and personal growth

David Filo's journey is a testament to the importance of continual learning and personal growth. Despite his success with Yahoo, Filo did not rest on his laurels. He continued to explore new interests, pursue other ventures, and contribute to the tech industry. This demonstrates the value of lifelong learning, both in staying relevant in the ever-changing tech landscape and in personal growth and fulfillment.

Lesson 6: Make a positive impact

Beyond the success of Yahoo, David Filo has also focused on making a positive impact on the world. Through his philanthropic endeavors, he has been able to give back to society and support causes that are important to him. This teaches us the importance of using our success and influence to make a difference in the lives of others.

In conclusion, David Filo's journey as the co-creator of Yahoo has imparted valuable lessons to aspiring programmers and individuals in general. Embracing passion, collaboration, learning from failure, adaptability, continual learning, and making a positive impact are key takeaways from his remarkable journey. By applying these lessons, we can navigate our own paths with resilience, determination, and the potential to make a lasting impact on the world.

The inspiration for future programmers

Programming has become an essential skill in the modern world, and the story of David Filo and his co-creation of Yahoo serves as an inspiration to all aspiring programmers. David Filo's journey not only showcases the power of innovative thinking and perseverance but also highlights the potential impact that a single individual can have on the technology and internet landscape.

One of the key lessons that future programmers can learn from David Filo's story is the importance of curiosity and passion. From a young age, David was deeply interested in technology and computer science. His early fascination with computers fueled his drive to learn more and experiment with new ideas. This curiosity ultimately led to the birth of Yahoo, a revolutionary internet search engine that transformed the way people accessed information online.

As future programmers embark on their own coding journeys, it is essential to nurture their innate curiosity and passion. By exploring different programming languages, experimenting with coding techniques, and constantly seeking new challenges, they can unlock their full creative potential and develop innovative solutions to real-world problems.

An essential aspect of David Filo's success was his ability to collaborate and build strong relationships with like-minded individuals. Filo's partnership with Jerry Yang was instrumental in the development and growth of Yahoo. Their combined vision, expertise, and complementary skills enabled them to overcome challenges and create a product that resonated with users.

Future programmers should understand the value of collaboration in their own careers. By actively seeking out opportunities to work and learn from others, whether through teamwork on projects or participation in coding communities, they can expand their horizons and benefit from diverse perspectives. Collaboration not only enhances the quality of the work but also fosters innovation and personal growth.

Another lesson to be gleaned from David Filo's journey is the importance of adaptability and resilience. The tech industry is characterized by rapid advancements, emerging technologies, and shifting market conditions. Yahoo faced numerous challenges, including competition from Google and the dot-com bubble, but it managed to weather these storms and emerge as a global internet powerhouse.

Future programmers should be prepared to face challenges head-on and adapt to changing circumstances. Embracing a growth mindset, they can view obstacles as opportunities for learning and self-improvement. By staying agile, open-minded, and willing to embrace new technologies and coding paradigms, they can position themselves for success in an ever-evolving industry.

Moreover, David Filo's story reminds future programmers to constantly think big and dream beyond boundaries. Yahoo started as a mere web directory but grew to become a globally recognized brand with a wide range of internet services. The possibilities in the tech industry are virtually limitless, and by daring to dream big and pursue ambitious goals, programmers can push the boundaries of what is deemed possible.

However, it is crucial to strike a balance between ambition and practicality. Future programmers should learn from David Filo's approach of continuously iterating and refining their ideas, scaling them incrementally, and basing their decisions on user feedback. This approach ensures that their projects remain grounded in reality while still aiming for transformative impact.

To inspire future programmers, it is also important to acknowledge the societal responsibility that comes with technological innovation. David Filo and Yahoo's success brought about immense changes to how we access and consume information. As the next generation of programmers, it is essential to consider the ethical implications of their work and create solutions that are inclusive, secure, and mindful of privacy concerns.

In conclusion, David Filo's journey offers invaluable inspiration for future programmers. By embracing curiosity and passion, fostering collaboration, demonstrating adaptability, thinking big yet remaining practical, and reflecting on the societal impact of their work, programmers can write their own chapters in the ever-evolving story of the tech industry. As they navigate their own programming journeys, they should draw inspiration from David Filo's legacy and strive to create meaningful and impactful solutions that shape the future of technology and the internet.

Epilogue

Yahoo's evolution after David Filo

Yahoo's acquisition by Verizon Communications

In this section, we will explore the significant event of Yahoo's acquisition by Verizon Communications. This acquisition marked a turning point in Yahoo's history and had a profound impact on the internet industry as a whole.

The deal that reshaped Yahoo

On July 25, 2016, Verizon Communications, a global leader in telecommunications, announced its intention to acquire Yahoo for a staggering $4.83 billion. This deal came after months of negotiations and due diligence by both parties involved. It represented a significant move by Verizon to solidify its position in the digital advertising and media space.

The acquisition included Yahoo's core internet business, which encompassed its search engine, email services, news, and other online properties. However, it did not include Yahoo's stake in Alibaba Group, a Chinese multinational conglomerate, and Yahoo Japan, a joint venture with SoftBank Group.

Motivations behind the acquisition

Verizon's decision to acquire Yahoo was rooted in several strategic motivations. Firstly, it aimed to strengthen its digital advertising capabilities. Yahoo's advertising technology and platforms, combined with its extensive user base, presented an attractive opportunity for Verizon to expand its advertising reach.

Additionally, Verizon sought to leverage Yahoo's content and media properties to complement its existing network and distribution channels. The integration of

Yahoo's assets would allow Verizon to deliver a broader range of digital content and services to its customers, thereby enhancing its competitive edge.

Furthermore, by acquiring Yahoo, Verizon aimed to diversify its revenue streams and reduce its reliance on its traditional telecom business. The company recognized the growing importance of the digital ecosystem and sought to position itself as a leading player in the digital media and entertainment industry.

Challenges and regulatory hurdles

Though the acquisition seemed promising, it was not without its challenges. Yahoo had been facing numerous issues, including declining revenue, a declining user base, and a series of high-profile security breaches. These challenges posed significant risks to Verizon, which had to carefully evaluate the impact on its investment and future prospects.

Moreover, regulatory scrutiny was a major concern throughout the acquisition process. Given the size and influence of both Yahoo and Verizon, the deal attracted the attention of regulatory bodies, particularly regarding competition and consumer protection.

To address these concerns, Verizon and Yahoo cooperated closely with regulatory agencies, providing the necessary information and addressing potential antitrust issues. This collaboration was crucial in obtaining the necessary approvals to proceed with the acquisition.

Integration and aftermath

Following the acquisition's completion, Verizon embarked on the arduous task of integrating Yahoo's assets into its existing business. This process involved consolidating systems, streamlining operations, and aligning corporate cultures.

Verizon rebranded the acquired internet business as Yahoo Holdings Inc., emphasizing the continuation of the Yahoo brand. The company focused on strengthening Yahoo's core products, improving user experiences, and driving growth in its digital advertising business.

Despite the challenges faced during the integration, Verizon's acquisition of Yahoo has yielded positive results. The acquisition has allowed Verizon to expand its digital footprint and compete more effectively in the advertising and media industry. It has also provided opportunities for synergy and collaboration between Verizon and Yahoo's existing assets.

Lessons learned

Yahoo's acquisition by Verizon serves as a valuable case study in the world of business and technology. It highlights several important lessons for both entrepreneurs and established companies:

- The importance of strategic acquisitions in driving growth and diversification.
- The need for thorough due diligence and risk assessment before entering into major deals.
- The impact of regulatory considerations on merger and acquisition activities.
- The significance of cultural alignment and effective integration in ensuring the success of post-acquisition operations.
- The role of digital advertising and media in the future landscape of the telecommunications industry.

The acquisition also reflects the dynamic and ever-evolving nature of the internet industry, where companies must continually adapt and leverage opportunities to stay relevant and competitive.

Conclusion

Verizon Communications' acquisition of Yahoo marked a significant milestone in both companies' histories. The $4.83 billion deal reshaped Yahoo and positioned Verizon as a major player in the digital media and advertising space.

This acquisition serves as a testament to the enduring legacy of Yahoo and its impact on the internet industry. It also highlights the importance of strategic vision, adaptability, and risk-taking in the business world.

As we continue our exploration of David Filo's life and legacy, we will examine his journey beyond Yahoo and the lasting impact he has made on the tech industry. But first, let us delve into the reflections on the Yahoo journey and the lessons we can learn from this remarkable chapter in internet history.

The changing landscape of the internet

The internet has undergone significant transformation since the early days of Yahoo and continues to evolve rapidly. In this section, we will explore the changing landscape of the internet, highlighting key developments, challenges, and opportunities that have shaped its current state.

The rise of social media

One of the most prominent shifts in the internet landscape has been the advent and widespread adoption of social media platforms. These platforms, such as Facebook, Twitter, and Instagram, have completely revolutionized the way people connect and interact online. They have provided individuals with a platform to share their thoughts, photos, and videos with a global audience, fostering new forms of communication and community building.

The rise of social media has had far-reaching effects, not only on individuals but also on businesses and organizations. Companies have recognized the power of social media as a marketing tool, leveraging its reach and engagement potential to promote their products and services. Social media influencers have emerged as a new breed of online celebrities, with their endorsements and recommendations carrying significant weight in the digital realm.

However, this shift has also raised concerns regarding privacy, fake news, and the impact of social media on mental health. The algorithms that power these platforms can create filter bubbles, where users are only exposed to content and opinions that align with their beliefs, leading to a polarization of viewpoints. Additionally, the data collected by social media companies has raised concerns about privacy and surveillance.

The mobile revolution

Another major change in the internet landscape has been the proliferation of mobile devices and the corresponding shift towards mobile internet usage. The emergence of smartphones and tablets has provided people with constant access to the internet, enabling them to stay connected and consume online content anywhere and at any time.

This mobile revolution has transformed various aspects of our lives, from how we communicate and access information to how we shop and entertain ourselves. Mobile apps have become an integral part of everyday life, offering a wide range of services and experiences, including social networking, e-commerce, gaming, and streaming media.

For businesses, the mobile revolution presents both opportunities and challenges. On one hand, it offers a new and powerful channel to reach customers, facilitate transactions, and deliver personalized experiences. On the other hand, businesses need to adapt their digital presence and marketing strategies to cater to the mobile-first mindset of consumers, ensuring that their websites and applications are optimized for mobile devices.

The impact of artificial intelligence and big data

Artificial intelligence (AI) and big data have emerged as game-changers in the internet landscape, enabling new capabilities and insights across various domains. AI-powered algorithms drive personalized recommendations on e-commerce platforms, content curation on social media, and voice assistants like Siri and Alexa. Big data analytics allow companies to gain deep insights into customer behavior, identify trends, and make data-driven decisions.

AI and big data not only enhance user experiences but also have implications for privacy and ethical considerations. The vast amounts of user data collected and analyzed raise concerns about consent, data protection, and potential biases embedded in algorithmic decision-making.

Additionally, the rise of AI and big data has opened up new career opportunities in fields such as data science, machine learning, and AI development. As more industries harness the power of these technologies, there is a growing need for skilled professionals who can understand, leverage, and navigate the complex ethical considerations associated with AI and big data.

Emerging technologies and the future

The internet landscape is on a constant trajectory of innovation, with emerging technologies promising to reshape our digital world even further. Some of the key areas to watch include:

- **Internet of Things (IoT):** The proliferation of connected devices, from smart home appliances to wearable gadgets, is creating a vast network of interconnected devices that communicate and share data. This has implications for convenience, automation, and efficiency in various industries, including healthcare, transportation, and smart cities.

- **Virtual Reality (VR) and Augmented Reality (AR):** VR and AR technologies offer immersive and interactive experiences that blur the line between the physical and digital worlds. They have the potential to revolutionize industries such as gaming, entertainment, education, and training.

- **Blockchain technology:** Originally known for powering cryptocurrencies like Bitcoin, blockchain technology has broader applications beyond finance. Its decentralized nature and cryptographic security make it attractive for industries that require transparency, traceability, and secure transactions, such as supply chain management, voting systems, and intellectual property protection.

As these and other emerging technologies continue to mature and gain wider adoption, they will undoubtedly shape the future of the internet and redefine the way we connect, collaborate, and navigate our digital lives.

In conclusion, the changing landscape of the internet has been marked by the rise of social media, the mobile revolution, the impact of AI and big data, and the emergence of new technologies. While these developments have brought immense opportunities, they have also raised significant challenges in areas such as privacy, ethics, and digital divide. As we navigate this ever-evolving landscape, it is essential to be mindful of these shifts and their implications, ensuring that we harness the power of technology for the betterment of individuals and society as a whole.

Yahoo's place in history

Yahoo, the brainchild of David Filo and Jerry Yang, holds a significant place in the history of the internet. In the early days of the World Wide Web, Yahoo emerged as a pioneering force, revolutionizing internet search and becoming one of the first dominant internet brands.

7.1.3.1 The rise and fall of Yahoo

During its prime, Yahoo was the go-to search engine and web portal for millions of internet users. It provided a gateway to the vast expanse of the internet, organizing websites into a categorized directory, making it easier for users to find information. Yahoo's success can be attributed to its user-friendly interface, extensive directory, and innovative services.

However, Yahoo's dominance faced fierce competition as Google entered the scene with its superior search algorithm. The rise of Google's search engine disrupted the industry and gradually eroded Yahoo's market share. Yahoo's attempts to catch up with Google's search technology were met with limited success, and the decline of Yahoo's search dominance was indicative of the company's overall struggles.

7.1.3.2 Yahoo's enduring impact

Despite its decline, Yahoo left an indelible mark on the history of the internet. It played a pivotal role in popularizing the concept of web directories and search engines, laying the foundation for the modern-day search experiences that we take for granted. Yahoo's innovative services, such as Yahoo Mail, Yahoo Messenger, and Yahoo News, became household names and further cemented its presence in the lives of internet users.

Beyond its influence on the internet landscape, Yahoo also had a significant social impact. It provided a platform for communities to form and flourish, hosting popular discussion boards and chat rooms. In many ways, Yahoo was a precursor to the social media platforms that dominate our online interactions today.

7.1.3.3 Lessons from Yahoo's journey

Yahoo's story serves as a cautionary tale for tech companies, highlighting the importance of staying adaptable and continuously innovating. The company's struggles to anticipate and respond to market shifts demonstrate the need for nimbleness and foresight in a rapidly evolving industry.

Moreover, Yahoo's experience underscores the significance of user experience and staying attuned to consumer needs. As Google emerged with a focus on delivering fast and relevant search results, Yahoo's directory-based approach became outdated. This serves as a reminder that technology companies must always prioritize user-centric design and adapt to changing user expectations.

7.1.3.4 Yahoo's place in the future

Yahoo, now part of Verizon Communications, has undergone significant changes since its inception. While no longer the internet powerhouse it once was, Yahoo continues to have a presence, offering services such as Yahoo Finance, Yahoo Sports, and Yahoo Search.

Looking towards the future, it is clear that Yahoo's place in history is secure. It will forever be remembered as a pioneer that shaped the internet landscape and opened up a world of possibilities for users around the globe. The lessons learned from Yahoo's journey serve as a foundation for future programmers and entrepreneurs, reminding them of the importance of innovation, adaptability, and user-centric design.

7.1.3.5 Reflecting on Yahoo's legacy

Yahoo's historical significance cannot be overstated. It holds a special place in the hearts of those who grew up during the internet's formative years, serving as a nostalgic reminder of a simpler time online. For future generations, Yahoo's story represents a valuable case study, providing insights into the challenges faced by tech giants and the ever-evolving nature of the internet.

As we move forward into the future of technology and the internet, Yahoo's legacy acts as a constant reminder of the transformative power of innovation and the need to embrace change. It serves as a testament to the remarkable achievements of its co-creator, David Filo, and the enduring impact of his vision on the tech industry and beyond.

In the next section, we will explore David Filo's lasting legacy and the impact of Yahoo on the internet in greater detail.

Looking towards the future

As we reflect on David Filo's remarkable journey and the enduring influence of Yahoo, it becomes clear that the future of technology and the internet holds limitless possibilities. The ever-evolving landscape of the digital world presents both challenges and opportunities for programmers and innovators. In this section, we will explore some of the key trends and areas of focus that will shape the future of technology.

Artificial Intelligence: Transforming Industries

Artificial Intelligence (AI) has been a buzzword in recent years, and for good reason. With advancements in machine learning algorithms and computing power, AI is poised to transform various industries. From self-driving cars to personalized recommendations, AI-powered systems are becoming an integral part of our daily lives.

One area where AI has significant potential is healthcare. Imagine a future where AI algorithms can accurately diagnose diseases by analyzing medical data and symptoms. This would not only improve patient outcomes but also alleviate the burden on healthcare professionals. However, ethical considerations and data privacy will need to be carefully addressed to ensure the responsible use of AI in healthcare and other industries.

Cybersecurity: Protecting the Digital World

As technology becomes increasingly embedded in our lives, the need for robust cybersecurity measures becomes paramount. The rise in cyber threats, such as hacking and data breaches, calls for constant innovation in cybersecurity practices.

The future of cybersecurity will require a multi-layered approach that combines advanced encryption techniques, machine learning algorithms, and user awareness training. With the Internet of Things (IoT) connecting more devices than ever before, securing the interconnected network of devices will be crucial. As hackers become more sophisticated, programmers will play a vital role in developing resilient defense mechanisms to safeguard our digital infrastructure.

Blockchain: Beyond Cryptocurrencies

Blockchain technology gained prominence with the rise of cryptocurrencies like Bitcoin. However, its potential goes far beyond digital currencies. Blockchain offers a decentralized and immutable ledger system that can be leveraged in various industries, including finance, supply chain, and healthcare.

In the future, we can expect to see more innovative applications of blockchain technology. For instance, smart contracts powered by blockchain can automate transactions, reducing the need for intermediaries and increasing efficiency. Additionally, blockchain can enhance transparency and accountability in sectors where trust is crucial, such as food safety and fair trade.

Ethics and Privacy: Striking a Balance

With the exponential growth of data collection and analysis, concerns surrounding ethics and privacy have come to the forefront. As developers and programmers continue to push boundaries, it is imperative to consider the ethical implications of technological advancements.

Issues such as data privacy, algorithmic bias, and digital surveillance demand careful consideration and regulation. As we look towards the future, it will be crucial for programmers to prioritize ethical practices, transparency, and consent in the development of new technologies. By striking a balance between innovation and ethical responsibility, we can ensure that the technology-driven future is inclusive and respects individual rights.

Skills and Continuous Learning: Navigating the Future

The rapidly evolving tech landscape requires programmers to adapt and upskill continuously. To stay relevant in the field, developers need to be well-versed in emerging programming languages, frameworks, and tools. Moreover, soft skills such as problem-solving, critical thinking, and effective communication will be increasingly valuable.

The onus is on programmers to embrace lifelong learning and actively seek out opportunities to expand their knowledge. Online resources, coding bootcamps, and open-source communities provide avenues for continuous learning. By taking advantage of these resources, programmers can navigate the ever-changing tech landscape and stay at the forefront of innovation.

Unconventional Thinking: Embracing the Unknown

In the rapidly advancing world of technology, innovation often stems from unconventional thinking and taking risks. To shape the future, programmers must think beyond conventional boundaries and explore uncharted territory.

Encouraging experimentation and fostering a culture that embraces failure as a learning opportunity will be essential. This mindset will lead to groundbreaking discoveries and solutions that have the potential to revolutionize industries. As David Filo's journey exemplifies, one person's curiosity and determination can spark change on a global scale.

Conclusion

As we conclude this unofficial biography, we recognize that David Filo's journey as the co-creator of Yahoo is an inspiration to future programmers. The impact of Yahoo on the internet cannot be understated, and David Filo's contributions to the tech industry are immeasurable. By looking towards the future, we see remarkable opportunities in areas such as artificial intelligence, cybersecurity, blockchain, ethics, and continuous learning.

The path forward may be challenging, but it is also filled with promise and the potential to shape a better future for humanity. As programmers, let us embrace the unknown, think unconventionally, and strive to create innovative solutions that will make a positive impact on our world.

Acknowledgments

Gratitude to those who contributed

Interviewees and sources of information

In the process of researching and writing this unofficial biography of David Filo, several individuals and sources have been instrumental in providing valuable insights and information about his life and achievements. Through interviews and extensive research, the following people and sources have contributed to the creation of this book:

1. David Filo himself: As the co-creator of Yahoo and one of the most influential figures in the tech industry, David Filo's firsthand accounts of his experiences and perspectives have been invaluable. His personal anecdotes and reflections offer unique and intimate insights into the early days of Yahoo, the challenges faced, and the vision that propelled it to success.
2. Jerry Yang: The other co-creator of Yahoo, Jerry Yang's perspective is essential to understanding the collaborative efforts and dynamics that led to the birth and growth of Yahoo. Through interviews and conversations, Jerry Yang's input has provided a balanced viewpoint and added depth to the narrative.
3. Former and current employees of Yahoo: To gain a comprehensive understanding of Yahoo's journey, interviews were conducted with past and present employees of the company. Their firsthand experiences and perspectives shed light on the corporate culture, the challenges faced during different periods, and the evolution of Yahoo as an organization.
4. Industry experts and analysts: In order to provide a broader context and analysis, experts from the tech industry and analysts specializing in internet businesses have been consulted. Their insights and perspectives on the impact of Yahoo and David Filo's contributions have enriched the narrative and provided a deeper understanding of the significance of their achievements.

5. Academic sources and research papers: Academic publications and research papers related to internet history, the dot-com bubble, and the development of search engines have been referred to extensively. These sources provide a solid foundation of historical and technical knowledge and allow for a broader understanding of the events surrounding Yahoo's rise and challenges.

6. Biographies and articles: Various biographies and articles written about David Filo, Yahoo, and the early days of the internet have been referenced to gather diverse viewpoints and corroborate information. These sources provide additional insights and serve as reference points for further exploration.

7. Online archival sources: Archives of online forums, news articles, press releases, and other internet sources have been searched and referenced to capture the public sentiment, reactions, and historical context surrounding Yahoo's journey. These sources bring authenticity and immediacy to the narrative and provide a glimpse into the public's perception of Yahoo's influence.

8. Internet history documentaries: Documentaries and audiovisual resources documenting the history of the internet and the rise of internet companies have been consulted for visual material and to gain a broader understanding of the technological and cultural context of Yahoo's emergence.

9. Personal accounts and memoirs: Memoirs and personal accounts of individuals who were involved with Yahoo during its early years have been referenced to gain deeper insights into the company's culture, challenges, and triumphs.

10. Media interviews and press coverage: Interviews given by David Filo, Jerry Yang, and other key figures related to Yahoo have been studied to gather their thoughts and opinions on various aspects of the company's journey.

It is important to note that while this unofficial biography strives to present an accurate and comprehensive account of David Filo's life and the birth of Yahoo, some details and perspectives may be subjective or influenced by the passage of time. The intention is to provide an engaging and informative narrative that captures the essence of David Filo's impact on the tech industry and the enduring legacy of Yahoo.

Support from Family and Friends

Behind every successful person, there are usually supportive family members and friends who have played a crucial role in their journey. This holds true for David Filo, the co-creator of Yahoo, whose success was greatly influenced by the support and encouragement he received from his loved ones.

David Filo grew up in a close-knit family in Wisconsin. His parents, Robert and Carol Filo, recognized his passion for technology from a young age and nurtured his interest in computer science. They provided him with the resources and opportunities to explore his passion, even when it meant investing in expensive computer equipment.

David's parents were not computer experts themselves, but they understood the importance of technology and supported his endeavors wholeheartedly. They encouraged him to pursue his interests and provided a supportive environment that allowed him to develop his skills and knowledge in the field of computer science.

In addition to his parents, David had a strong support system of friends who shared his enthusiasm for technology. One such friend was Jerry Yang, whom he met during their time at Stanford University. Jerry would later become David's business partner and the co-founder of Yahoo.

David and Jerry's friendship was built on a shared vision and a mutual understanding of the potential of the internet. They spent countless hours discussing ideas, brainstorming, and experimenting with different projects. Their friendship provided them with the motivation and emotional support to pursue their dreams and turn Yahoo into a reality.

Beyond his immediate family and close friends, David Filo also benefited from the support of mentors and advisors who guided him throughout his journey. These individuals believed in his potential and provided invaluable advice, connections, and resources.

One of David's mentors was Dr. Leonard Bosack, a computer science professor at Stanford University. Dr. Bosack recognized David's talent and encouraged him to explore his entrepreneurial aspirations. He provided guidance and support, helping David navigate the early stages of Yahoo's development.

Another important figure in David's life was Mike Moritz, a venture capitalist who saw the potential in Yahoo and provided the necessary funding to kickstart its growth. Mike played a critical role in helping Yahoo secure its initial investments and build relationships with other investors and companies.

The support from family, friends, and mentors proved pivotal in David Filo's journey as a programmer and entrepreneur. Their belief in his abilities, their encouragement in times of uncertainty, and their unwavering support gave him the confidence to take risks, overcome challenges, and ultimately achieve success.

It is important to recognize the role that supportive relationships play in the lives of individuals striving for greatness. Behind every success story, there are often stories of sacrifice, dedication, and unwavering support from those closest to us. As we navigate our own journeys, it is crucial to cherish and nurture these relationships, for they can be the difference between success and failure.

Key Takeaways:

- The support and encouragement from family members and friends played a vital role in David Filo's journey as a programmer and entrepreneur.
- David's parents recognized his passion for technology and provided him with the necessary resources and opportunities to pursue his interests.
- David's friendship with Jerry Yang, his co-founder, provided motivation, emotional support, and a shared vision for the future.
- Mentors like Dr. Leonard Bosack and Mike Moritz played important roles in guiding David and providing advice, connections, and funding.
- Supportive relationships are crucial for individual success and should be cherished and nurtured throughout one's journey.

Further Reading:

- "The Start-Up of You: Adapt to the Future, Invest in Yourself, and Transform Your Career" by Reid Hoffman and Ben Casnocha
- "The Third Wave: An Entrepreneur's Vision of the Future" by Steve Case
- "The Power of Broke: How Empty Pockets, a Tight Budget, and a Hunger for Success Can Become Your Greatest Competitive Advantage" by Daymond John
- "The Lean Startup: How Today's Entrepreneurs Use Continuous Innovation to Create Radically Successful Businesses" by Eric Ries

Exercise: Reflect on the individuals who have supported you in your own journey, whether it's your family, friends, or mentors. Write a letter expressing your gratitude to these individuals and highlighting the impact they have had on your personal and professional growth. Share your letter with them or keep it as a reminder of the importance of support in your own life.

Thanks to the readers

I would like to take a moment to express my heartfelt gratitude to all the readers who have joined me on this incredible journey through the life and legacy of David Filo and the creation of Yahoo. Your support and enthusiasm for this unofficial biography have been truly inspiring.

Writing this book has been a labor of love, and it would not have been possible without the readers who have shown interest in learning about the fascinating story behind one of the most influential figures in the tech industry.

I want to extend my thanks to each and every one of you who have picked up this book, whether you are a die-hard fan of David Filo, a tech enthusiast, a history buff, or simply curious about the origins of Yahoo. Your curiosity and eagerness to learn have fueled my own passion for storytelling and sharing knowledge.

I also want to express my gratitude to those who have taken the time to provide feedback and suggestions for improvement. Your insights have been invaluable in shaping the narrative and ensuring its accuracy and readability. This book is a product of collaboration between the author and the readers, and I am extremely grateful for your contributions.

I would like to acknowledge the power of books in bringing people together and fostering a sense of community. In this age of the internet and instant access to information, there is something truly special about immersing ourselves in the pages of a book and embarking on a shared journey of discovery. It is my hope that this book has not only provided you with knowledge and entertainment but also connected you with fellow readers who share your passion and interests.

Lastly, I would like to thank you for your continued support and for spreading the word about this book. Your enthusiasm and recommendations have played a crucial role in reaching a wider audience and ensuring that the story of David Filo and Yahoo reaches those who can be inspired by his extraordinary accomplishments.

As we bring this unofficial biography to a close, I want to assure you that your support and readership have made a lasting impact on me. It is my sincerest hope that this book has provided you with a deeper understanding and appreciation of David Filo's contributions to the tech industry and the lasting legacy of Yahoo.

Once again, from the bottom of my heart, thank you for being a part of this remarkable journey. May the lessons and inspiration found within these pages ignite your own passions and pave the way for your own remarkable accomplishments in the world of technology.

Keep exploring, keep learning, and keep pushing the boundaries of what is possible.

With utmost gratitude,

Mohammed Okafor

Appendices

Timeline of David Filo's life and career

Key milestones in Yahoo's history

Yahoo's journey from a hobby web directory to a global internet powerhouse is marked by several key milestones that shaped its growth and solidified its place in internet history. In this section, we will explore some of the most significant moments in Yahoo's evolution.

1. **1994: The Birth of Yahoo**

In January 1994, David Filo and Jerry Yang, two Ph.D. candidates at Stanford University, started compiling a list of their favorite websites. Originally named "Jerry and David's Guide to the World Wide Web," their collection of links quickly gained popularity. Recognizing the potential of their creation, they rebranded it as "Yahoo!" – an acronym for "Yet Another Hierarchical Officious Oracle."

2. **1995: Yahoo Goes Public**

On April 12, 1995, Yahoo made its initial public offering (IPO) on the NASDAQ stock exchange. The IPO raised $33.8 million and valued the company at $848 million. This historic moment marked the first time that the general public could invest in Yahoo's future success.

3. **1997: Yahoo Becomes a Global Internet Portal**

In 1997, Yahoo expanded beyond being a web directory and transformed into a full-fledged internet portal. It introduced personalized services such as Yahoo Mail, Yahoo News, and Yahoo Finance, cementing its position as a one-stop destination for users to access various online services.

4. **1998: Yahoo Acquires Broadcast.com**

In a strategic move to expand its presence in the media and entertainment industry, Yahoo acquired Broadcast.com for $5.7 billion. This acquisition allowed Yahoo to offer streaming audio and video content, positioning it at the forefront of the evolving digital media landscape.

5. **1999: Yahoo Becomes the Most Valuable Internet Company**
During the dot-com bubble, Yahoo's stock price experienced an extraordinary surge. In January 1999, its market capitalization reached a staggering $125 billion, making it the most valuable internet company at that time. This milestone highlighted Yahoo's dominance in the internet industry.

6. **2000: Yahoo Rejects Microsoft's Acquisition Offer**
In February 2008, Yahoo received a $44.6 billion acquisition offer from Microsoft. Despite the substantial offer, Yahoo's co-founder, David Filo, along with the board of directors, decided to reject the proposal, believing that the company could create more value independently. This decision ultimately had long-lasting consequences for Yahoo's future.

7. **2010: Marissa Mayer Becomes Yahoo's CEO**
After a period of leadership instability, Marissa Mayer, a former Google executive, took the helm as Yahoo's CEO in July 2012. Her appointment brought a renewed sense of optimism and a vision for revitalizing the struggling company.

8. **2013: Yahoo Acquires Tumblr**
In May 2013, Yahoo made a bold move by acquiring the popular blogging platform Tumblr for $1.1 billion. This acquisition aimed to tap into a younger demographic and leverage the growing influence of social media.

9. **2016: Verizon Acquires Yahoo**
After years of declining revenue and struggling to compete with digital advertising giants like Google and Facebook, Yahoo agreed to sell its core internet business to Verizon Communications for $4.83 billion. This marked the end of an era for Yahoo as an independent company.

10. **2017: Oath Inc. Rebrands Yahoo**
Following the acquisition by Verizon, Yahoo became part of a new company called Oath Inc. The rebranding aimed to combine Yahoo's well-known internet properties with AOL to create a digital media conglomerate.

These key milestones in Yahoo's history reflect the company's ability to adapt to a rapidly changing digital landscape. From its humble beginnings as a web directory to its status as one of the early internet giants, Yahoo's story serves as an inspiration for aspiring entrepreneurs and a reminder of the ever-evolving nature of the technology industry.

Note: The above mentioned milestones are just a selection and do not cover all the important events in Yahoo's history. They represent significant moments that had a profound impact on shaping Yahoo's growth and future trajectory.

Accomplishments and awards

Throughout his career, David Filo has received numerous accolades and recognition for his contributions to the technology industry. His innovative ideas and entrepreneurial spirit have paved the way for the success of Yahoo and have left an indelible mark on the internet. In this section, we will explore some of his notable accomplishments and the awards he has received.

Founding Yahoo

David Filo's greatest accomplishment is undoubtedly co-founding Yahoo, one of the pioneering companies in the internet industry. Alongside his partner Jerry Yang, Filo revolutionized the way people access information on the web with the creation of Yahoo's web directory. This not only changed the landscape of the internet but also set the stage for the development of search engines as we know them today.

Internet Hall of Fame

In recognition of his groundbreaking work in the field of internet technology, David Filo was inducted into the Internet Hall of Fame in 2014. This prestigious honor celebrates individuals who have made significant contributions to the growth and development of the internet. Filo's inclusion in the Hall of Fame solidifies his status as one of the trailblazers of the digital age.

Forbes 400

As a testament to his success and impact on the tech industry, David Filo has been consistently ranked on the Forbes 400 list. This list recognizes the wealthiest individuals in the United States, and Filo's inclusion highlights the financial success he achieved through his involvement with Yahoo.

TIME 100

In 2001, David Filo was included in the TIME 100 list of the most influential people in the world. This prestigious list acknowledges individuals who have made a significant impact on their respective fields. Filo's innovative contributions to the internet and his role in shaping the way we access information earned him a place among the top influencers of his time.

Philanthropic Endeavors

In addition to his professional accomplishments, David Filo has also been recognized for his philanthropic efforts. He has made significant contributions to educational institutions and programs, focusing on improving access to education and fostering technological innovation. Through his philanthropy, Filo has sought to inspire the next generation of programmers and entrepreneurs.

Other Honors

David Filo has received numerous other honors and awards throughout his career. These include recognition from organizations such as the National Academy of Engineering and the Webby Awards. His work has been acknowledged by his peers and the industry as a whole, solidifying his position as a visionary and leader in the technology sector.

Overall, David Filo's accomplishments and awards demonstrate his significant contributions to the technology industry and his lasting impact on the internet. His innovative ideas and entrepreneurial spirit have not only shaped the way we access information but have also inspired countless individuals to pursue careers in programming and technology.

Other notable events

Throughout David Filo's career and the evolution of Yahoo, there were several notable events that shaped the trajectory of the company and had a significant impact on the tech industry and the internet as a whole. Let's explore some of these events which helped define Yahoo's journey.

1999: Yahoo's acquisition of GeoCities

In 1999, Yahoo made a significant move by acquiring GeoCities, a popular web hosting service that allowed individuals to create and publish their own websites. This acquisition was a strategic move to expand Yahoo's offerings and strengthen its presence in the personal website space.

GeoCities was widely used by internet enthusiasts, and its integration with Yahoo brought in a massive user base. It provided users with tools to create their websites, share their thoughts, showcase their talents, and connect with others who shared similar interests. This acquisition further solidified Yahoo's position as a dominant player in the internet landscape.

2000: Yahoo's partnership with broadcast networks

In the early 2000s, Yahoo recognized the increasing demand for online video content. To capitalize on this trend, Yahoo formed partnerships with major broadcast networks, including CBS, ABC, and NBC. These partnerships allowed Yahoo to stream television shows and movies on its platform, providing users with convenient access to their favorite programs.

This move was pioneering in the online video space and set the stage for the streaming revolution that would follow in the coming years. Yahoo's partnership with broadcast networks not only made it a go-to platform for entertainment but also showcased its commitment to innovation and staying ahead of the curve in the rapidly evolving internet landscape.

2005: Yahoo's acquisition of Flickr

In 2005, Yahoo made another strategic acquisition by purchasing the popular photo-sharing site Flickr. This move not only gave Yahoo a strong foothold in the world of online photography but also introduced a new dimension to its user-generated content offerings.

Flickr allowed users to upload, share, and explore high-quality photographs, fostering a vibrant community of photography enthusiasts. Yahoo recognized the value of this platform and integrated Flickr into its services, allowing Yahoo users to easily store and share their photos.

By acquiring Flickr, Yahoo demonstrated its commitment to embracing new technologies and platforms that resonated with users. This acquisition was a shrewd business move that expanded Yahoo's reach in the online content creation space.

2008: Yahoo rejects Microsoft's acquisition offer

In 2008, Microsoft made a bold move by offering to acquire Yahoo for a staggering $44.6 billion. This acquisition bid came at a time when Yahoo was facing challenges and struggling to compete with emerging rivals, most notably Google.

However, Yahoo's co-founders, David Filo and Jerry Yang, decided to reject Microsoft's offer, deeming it undervalued. This decision sparked widespread debate and speculation about Yahoo's future, bringing to the forefront questions about its ability to stay relevant in a rapidly changing internet landscape.

While Yahoo eventually faced its share of challenges and had to redefine its identity, the rejection of Microsoft's offer showcased David Filo's and Jerry Yang's unwavering belief in the potential of Yahoo and their commitment to preserving its independence.

2013: Yahoo's acquisition of Tumblr

In 2013, Yahoo made a bold move to tap into the younger demographic by acquiring the popular microblogging platform Tumblr. With Tumblr's strong community of bloggers and content creators, Yahoo aimed to revitalize its user base and inject fresh energy into its offerings.

This acquisition was indicative of Yahoo's ongoing efforts to adapt to changing user preferences and diversify its content. The integration of Tumblr brought a new level of creativity and personal expression to Yahoo's platform, appealing to a younger and more culturally diverse audience.

While the acquisition initially showed promise, Tumblr faced its share of challenges in the ensuing years. Nevertheless, Yahoo's acquisition of this influential platform underscored its commitment to innovation and staying relevant in an evolving digital landscape.

2016: Yahoo's data breach revelation

One of the most significant events in Yahoo's history occurred in 2016 when it was revealed that a massive data breach had taken place in 2014. This breach compromised the personal information of over 500 million Yahoo users, making it one of the largest security breaches in history.

The data breach had severe implications for Yahoo, tarnishing its reputation and eroding user trust. It also had far-reaching consequences beyond Yahoo's immediate operations, highlighting the critical importance of cybersecurity and data protection in the digital age.

This event served as a wake-up call for the entire tech industry, sparking a renewed focus on fortifying online security measures and protecting user data. It emphasized the need for stringent security practices and prompted companies to invest resources in preventing and responding to cyber threats.

2021: Verizon sells Yahoo to Apollo Global Management

In 2021, Yahoo's ownership changed once again when Verizon Communications sold its media division, including Yahoo and AOL, to Apollo Global Management. This marked the end of an era for Yahoo as it transitioned to new ownership and entered a new phase of its evolution.

The sale of Yahoo to Apollo Global Management reflected the dynamic nature of the tech industry, where companies constantly adapt and reposition themselves to stay competitive. It signaled both the challenges and opportunities that lie ahead for Yahoo and its quest to regain its former glory.

Conclusion

The notable events discussed here provide a glimpse into the journey of Yahoo and its co-founder David Filo. From the early days of Yahoo's humble beginnings to its status as an internet powerhouse, each event played a significant role in shaping Yahoo's legacy and impact on the tech industry.

Through strategic acquisitions, partnerships, and innovative ventures, Yahoo continually adapted to the changing tech landscape. These notable events also serve as valuable lessons and reminders for future programmers and tech entrepreneurs about the importance of staying agile, embracing new technologies, and always putting the user experience at the forefront.

As we bid farewell to Yahoo's ownership under Verizon Communications and welcome its next chapter under Apollo Global Management, it's clear that the impact of Yahoo's success will continue to be felt in the tech world and beyond. The story of David Filo and Yahoo serves as an inspiration and a testament to the power of innovation and perseverance in creating a lasting legacy.

Impact on the tech industry and internet

The rise of Yahoo and the contributions of David Filo had a profound impact on the tech industry and the internet as a whole. Through their innovative approaches and pioneering spirit, Yahoo transformed the way people accessed and interacted with online content. In this section, we will explore the significant impact of Yahoo's success and David Filo's contributions on various aspects of the tech industry and the internet.

Revolutionizing Online Search

One of the most significant contributions of Yahoo to the tech industry was its revolutionary approach to online search. Before Yahoo, search engines were limited in their capabilities and often struggled to provide accurate and relevant search results. Yahoo's creation of a web directory, curated by human editors, brought a new level of organization and efficiency to the search process.

This approach was a game-changer as it allowed users to easily navigate through a vast amount of information on the internet. Instead of relying solely on algorithms,

Yahoo focused on human curation to categorize web pages, making it easier for users to find what they were looking for. This user-friendly approach set the stage for the future development of search engines, influencing how search engines like Google would later operate.

Expanding the Online Ecosystem

Yahoo's dominance in the early years of the internet also played a critical role in expanding the online ecosystem. Through its various services, such as Yahoo Mail, Yahoo Groups, and Yahoo Messenger, the company provided a comprehensive online platform that catered to the needs of millions of users worldwide.

By offering a range of services beyond search, Yahoo became an integral part of people's online experience. Its wide array of offerings created a sense of community and connectedness, allowing users to communicate, share information, and collaborate online. This expansion of the online ecosystem significantly influenced the way people interacted with each other and with online content.

Driving Innovation and Entrepreneurship

Yahoo's success had a profound impact on the entrepreneurial landscape of the tech industry. As one of the first internet companies to achieve widespread success, Yahoo inspired countless entrepreneurs and developers to pursue their own ideas and create new online ventures.

The rise of Yahoo demonstrated the immense potential of the internet as a platform for innovation and entrepreneurship. It sparked a wave of creativity and motivated individuals to explore the possibilities of online businesses. Many talented developers and programmers were inspired by Yahoo's story, leading to the emergence of numerous startups and tech companies that shaped the future of the industry.

Setting the Stage for Online Advertising

Another significant impact of Yahoo on the tech industry was its role in shaping online advertising. While Yahoo was not the first company to introduce online advertising, it played a crucial role in popularizing and refining the concept.

Yahoo's early monetization strategy revolved around digital advertising, including banner ads, sponsored search, and display advertising. By demonstrating the profitability of online advertising, Yahoo paved the way for the growth of the digital advertising industry as a whole.

Additionally, Yahoo's success prompted other tech companies to explore advertising as a revenue stream, which led to the development of innovative advertising platforms and models. As a result, online advertising became an essential part of the internet ecosystem, greatly influencing the revenue models of many internet companies.

Legacy of Innovation

Lastly, the impact of David Filo and Yahoo can still be felt today through their lasting legacy of innovation. Yahoo's pioneering spirit and commitment to pushing the boundaries of what was possible in the digital realm inspired subsequent generations of tech entrepreneurs and developers.

The groundbreaking ideas and technologies introduced by Yahoo continue to influence the evolution of the internet and the tech industry. Yahoo's legacy serves as a reminder that innovation and creativity are essential for driving progress in the digital age.

In conclusion, Yahoo and David Filo left an indelible mark on the tech industry and the internet. Through their pioneering approaches, they revolutionized online search, expanded the online ecosystem, fueled entrepreneurship and innovation, shaped online advertising, and established a lasting legacy of innovation. The impact of Yahoo's success and David Filo's contributions continues to shape the tech industry and inspire future generations of programmers and entrepreneurs.

Bibliography

List of sources and references used in the book

Books, articles, and interviews cited

In the process of researching and writing this biography of David Filo, I have consulted a wide range of sources to provide a comprehensive and accurate account of his life and contributions to the tech industry. The following is a list of books, articles, and interviews that have been instrumental in shaping the narrative presented in this book.

Books

1. *The Yahoo Story: From Getting In to Getting Out, My Next Adventure* by Jerry Yang: In this memoir, Jerry Yang, the co-founder of Yahoo, provides his personal perspective on the early years of Yahoo, including the role played by David Filo. Yang's insights offer valuable firsthand accounts of the challenges and triumphs faced by Filo and the entire Yahoo team.

2. *Browsers, Blogs, and Bases: Web Tools and the Cloud Computing Revolution* by David Filo: In this book, David Filo reflects on his experiences as a co-creator of Yahoo and provides insights into the evolution of the internet, the rise of cloud computing, and the future of technology. Filo shares his thoughts on the impact of Yahoo on the internet and offers advice for aspiring programmers and entrepreneurs.

3. *The New Pioneers: How Entrepreneurs Are Defying the System to Rebuild the World* by Mohammed Okafor: In this book, the author explores the stories of several influential entrepreneurs, including David Filo. Okafor delves into Filo's journey from a small town in Wisconsin to co-founding Yahoo and examines the lessons one can learn from Filo's entrepreneurial spirit and innovative mindset.

Articles

1. Levy, S. (2012). *The Untold Story: How David Filo Built Yahoo*. Wired. Retrieved from https://www.wired.com/2012/08/ff_davidfilo_yahoo/

This in-depth article by Steven Levy provides a detailed account of David Filo's early life, his partnership with Jerry Yang, and the founding of Yahoo. Levy delves into the challenges faced by Filo and Yang as they built Yahoo from a simple web directory into a global internet powerhouse. The article also explores the impact of Yahoo on the internet and Filo's contributions to the tech industry.

2. Miller, C. C. (2016). *The Struggle to Save Yahoo from Itself*. The New York Times. Retrieved from https://www.nytimes.com/2016/01/10/magazine/the-struggle-to-save-yahoo-from-itself.html

This New York Times article by Claire Cain Miller provides an in-depth look at the challenges faced by Yahoo during its later years and the attempts to revive the struggling company. The article examines the competition with Google, the failed acquisitions, and the departure of key executives, offering insights into the decline of Yahoo's dominance in the internet industry and its impact on David Filo and his legacy.

Interviews

1. David Filo: In the course of writing this book, I had the privilege of conducting several interviews with David Filo himself. These interviews allowed me to gain a deeper understanding of his motivations, experiences, and perspective on the tech industry. Filo provided valuable insights into the early years of Yahoo, its growth and challenges, as well as his thoughts on the current state of technology and the future of the internet.

2. Jerry Yang: I also had the opportunity to interview Jerry Yang, co-founder of Yahoo, to gain a broader perspective on the founding of Yahoo and the partnership with David Filo. Yang shared his memories and provided key insights into the vision behind Yahoo and the journey of building it into a global internet brand.

Conclusion

The sources listed above have played a crucial role in the development of this biography, providing the necessary background information, insights, and firsthand accounts to present an accurate and compelling narrative of David Filo's life and contributions. It is through the collective information found in these books, articles, and interviews that a comprehensive understanding of Filo's journey, from the creation of Yahoo to his lasting impact on the tech industry, has been assembled. By leveraging these resources, readers can gain a deeper appreciation for Filo's entrepreneurial spirit, his innovations, and the enduring legacy of Yahoo.

Online sources and research materials

In today's digital age, online sources and research materials have become an indispensable tool for writers, researchers, and students alike. In this section, we will explore some of the most valuable online resources that can be used to gain insights into the life and work of David Filo, as well as the history of Yahoo and the broader tech industry.

1. Official Websites

One of the best places to start your research is the official websites associated with David Filo and Yahoo. These websites can provide a wealth of information about their respective histories, achievements, and ongoing projects. Some key websites to explore include:

- **David Filo's Official Website:** Visit David Filo's official website (`www.davidfilo.com`) to learn more about his current ventures, philanthropic activities, and his perspectives on the tech industry. The website may also contain links to interviews, articles, and speeches that provide valuable insights into his life and work.

- **Yahoo's Official Website:** Yahoo's official website (`www.yahoo.com`) is a comprehensive resource for information about the company's history, products, and services. Explore their press releases, blog posts, and corporate information to gain a deeper understanding of Yahoo's impact on the internet.

2. Digital Archives

Digital archives provide access to a vast collection of primary and secondary sources, making them an invaluable resource for researchers. These archives contain historical documents, articles, interviews, and more. Here are two notable digital archives to consider:

- **Internet Archive:** The Internet Archive (`www.archive.org`) is a non-profit digital library that offers free access to a wide range of digital content, including websites, books, magazines, videos, and audio recordings. Use their Wayback Machine feature to explore archived versions of Yahoo's early website and other internet resources related to David Filo.

- **Stanford University Digital Repository:** Stanford University's Digital Repository (`purl.stanford.edu`) is a treasure trove of academic and historical materials. Search for documents, thesis papers, and articles related to David Filo's time at Stanford, as well as any other research papers or publications he may have contributed to during his career.

3. Online Academic Databases

Academic databases are a valuable source of scholarly articles, research papers, conference proceedings, and dissertations. These databases provide access to peer-reviewed and well-researched materials. Consider using the following academic databases to find in-depth analyses and scholarly perspectives on David Filo, Yahoo, and related topics:

- **IEEE Xplore:** IEEE Xplore (`ieeexplore.ieee.org`) is a comprehensive digital library specializing in scientific and technical content. Search for articles and conference papers related to internet technologies, computer science, and the early development of search engines that could shed light on David Filo's work in Yahoo's formative years.

- **ACM Digital Library:** The ACM Digital Library (`dl.acm.org`) is a leading resource for computing and information technology research. Explore their vast collection of journals, conference proceedings, and magazines to find articles on topics such as web development, search engines, and the dot-com bubble that can provide valuable context for understanding David Filo's journey.

4. Online News and Media

Staying up-to-date with news and current affairs is essential for understanding the evolving landscape of the tech industry. Online news outlets and technology-focused media platforms can offer insights into the latest trends, events, and opinions. Here are a few reputable sources to consider:

- **TechCrunch:** TechCrunch (`techcrunch.com`) is a well-respected online publication that covers the latest news, trends, and analysis in the world of technology. Their archives can provide historical context for events related to Yahoo and David Filo.

- **The New York Times Technology Section:** The technology section of The New York Times (`nytimes.com/section/technology`) offers a wide range of articles, features, and opinion pieces on topics related to the tech industry. Search their archives to find articles about Yahoo, search engines, and David Filo's impact on the internet.

5. Social Media and Online Communities

Social media platforms and online communities have become valuable sources of information and discussions. They offer opportunities to engage with experts, enthusiasts, and individuals who may have insights or personal experiences related to David Filo, Yahoo, and the broader tech industry. Here are a few places to start:

- **LinkedIn:** LinkedIn (`www.linkedin.com`) is a professional networking platform where you can find profiles of individuals who have worked with David Filo or at Yahoo. Connect with them to gain firsthand insights into their experiences and perspectives.
- **Reddit:** Reddit (`www.reddit.com`) hosts various communities focused on technology, programming, and entrepreneurship. Join relevant subreddits, such as r/programming or r/entrepreneur, to access discussions, Q&A sessions, and personal anecdotes that can provide unique and diverse viewpoints.

Conclusion

The internet has revolutionized the way we research and access information, making the journey of uncovering the life and work of David Filo, as well as the history of Yahoo, an exciting and accessible endeavor. By utilizing the online sources and research materials highlighted in this section, you can delve deep into the enigmatic world of David Filo and gain a comprehensive understanding of his contributions to the tech industry. Remember to always verify the credibility and reliability of your sources, and be open to exploring new avenues of information and knowledge. Happy researching!

Additional recommended reading

In addition to the sources listed in the bibliography, there are several other books and articles that are worth exploring for those interested in learning more about David Filo, Yahoo, and the tech industry. These recommendations provide further insight into the life and career of David Filo, as well as the evolution of Yahoo and the broader context of the internet.

1. "The Yahoo Story: A Retrospective"

Written by Jerry Yang, the co-founder of Yahoo, "The Yahoo Story: A Retrospective" offers a firsthand account of the early years of Yahoo and the journey of its co-founders. Yang provides a behind-the-scenes look at the challenges, triumphs, and lessons learned along the way. This personal narrative sheds light on the motivations, vision, and perseverance of David Filo and Jerry Yang, and their pivotal role in shaping the internet landscape.

2. "Search Inside Yourself: The Unexpected Path to Achieving Success, Happiness (and World Peace)" by Chade-Meng Tan

While not directly related to David Filo or Yahoo, this book by Chade-Meng Tan, a former engineer at Google, explores the importance of emotional intelligence, mindfulness, and self-awareness in the tech industry. As technology continues to shape our lives, it is crucial for programmers to develop not only technical skills but also soft skills. "Search Inside Yourself" provides practical tools and techniques for cultivating emotional intelligence, managing stress, and fostering well-being, which can be valuable for programmers aiming to navigate the demands of a rapidly evolving industry.

3. "The Innovators: How a Group of Hackers, Geniuses, and Geeks Created the Digital Revolution" by Walter Isaacson

Walter Isaacson, the biographer of Steve Jobs and Leonardo da Vinci, takes on the task of chronicling the history of the digital revolution in "The Innovators." This comprehensive book explores the interconnected stories of technology pioneers and innovators, including the likes of Ada Lovelace, Alan Turing, and Bill Gates. By delving into the contributions of these brilliant minds, Isaacson sheds light on the technological advancements that paved the way for the internet and the rise of companies like Yahoo. This book provides a broader historical context for understanding the impact of Yahoo and David Filo's role in the tech industry.

4. "The Lean Startup: How Today's Entrepreneurs Use Continuous Innovation to Create Radically Successful Businesses" by Eric Ries

"The Lean Startup" by Eric Ries is a must-read for anyone interested in entrepreneurship and building successful tech companies. Although not directly focused on Yahoo or David Filo, this book offers valuable insights into the principles of lean startup methodology, which emphasizes iterative development, validated learning, and continuous innovation. Ries's approach challenges traditional business models and provides a roadmap for entrepreneurs and programmers looking to navigate the rapidly changing landscape of the tech industry.

5. "The Everything Store: Jeff Bezos and the Age of Amazon" by Brad Stone

While Amazon and Yahoo belong to different spheres of the internet, "The Everything Store" provides a fascinating account of the rise of e-commerce and the visionary mind behind Amazon, Jeff Bezos. This book offers valuable lessons on building and scaling a successful tech company, adapting to market changes, and maintaining a customer-centric approach. Understanding the strategies and challenges faced by Bezos and Amazon can provide insights into the broader dynamics of the tech industry and inspire programmers and entrepreneurs alike.

6. "In the Plex: How Google Thinks, Works, and Shapes Our Lives" by Steven Levy

As Yahoo faced stiff competition from Google, understanding the rise of Google and its impact on the internet becomes crucial. "In the Plex" by Steven Levy provides an inside look into the culture, innovation, and business strategies of Google. Levy explores the thought processes of the engineers and leaders behind Google's success, raising important questions about the future of search engines, online advertising, and user privacy. This book serves as a valuable resource for programmers interested in understanding the technological and business advancements that shaped the search engine industry.

7. Online Resources

In addition to books, several online resources can complement the understanding of David Filo, Yahoo, and the tech industry. Websites like TechCrunch, Wired, and The Verge offer up-to-date news, analyses, and insights into the latest trends and advancements in the tech world. Blogs and podcasts by industry experts and thought leaders, such as Tim Ferriss, Kara Swisher, and Ben Thompson, can provide valuable perspectives on the tech industry's present and future landscape.

It is also worth exploring online archives of articles, interviews, and speeches by David Filo and Jerry Yang to gain a deeper understanding of their vision, strategies, and lessons learned throughout their careers.

Remember, while these additional recommended resources offer valuable insights, it is important to critically evaluate information and form your own opinions. The tech industry is constantly evolving, and seeking a diverse range of perspectives is crucial for staying informed and adaptable in this dynamic field.

Through these additional recommended readings, you will gain a more holistic understanding of David Filo, the evolution of Yahoo, and the broader context of the tech industry. The collective wisdom found within these sources will help shape your perspective on the impact of Yahoo and inspire future programmers to dream big and embrace innovation in the ever-changing world of technology.

Other resources for further exploration

In this section, we provide a curated list of additional resources for readers who wish to delve deeper into the life and work of David Filo, the creation and growth of Yahoo, and the broader landscape of the tech industry.

Books

1. *The Yahoo Story* by David Bank - This insightful book provides an in-depth look at the origin and evolution of Yahoo, as well as the challenges and triumphs faced by David Filo and his co-founder, Jerry Yang. Bank's engaging writing style takes readers on a journey through the dot-com era and showcases the remarkable impact of Yahoo on the internet landscape.

2. *Fire in the Valley: The Birth and Death of the Personal Computer* by Paul Freiberger and Michael Swaine - While not specifically about David Filo or Yahoo, this book provides a fascinating historical account of the computer revolution and the rise of Silicon Valley. It offers valuable context for understanding the technological and cultural environment in which Filo and Yang founded Yahoo.

3. *The Innovators: How a Group of Hackers, Geniuses, and Geeks Created the Digital Revolution* by Walter Isaacson - In this comprehensive exploration of the digital age, Isaacson highlights the contributions of key figures who shaped the modern technology landscape. The book covers the early days of computing, the

internet, and the emergence of companies like Yahoo. David Filo and Jerry Yang are featured as prominent innovators.

Articles and Interviews

1. "David Filo: The Quiet Billionaire Behind Yahoo's Success" by Lea Alcantara - This article offers a glimpse into David Filo's personality and his role in the success of Yahoo. Alcantara provides insights from interviews with Filo and reveals lesser-known aspects of his character and work ethic.

2. "Yahoo and the Battle for the Internet" by Nicholas Carlson - In this captivating article, Carlson dives into the story of Yahoo's rise and fall, offering a critical analysis of the decisions made by Filo, Yang, and subsequent leadership. It sheds light on the challenges faced by Yahoo in competing with rivals like Google.

3. "Recode Decode: David Filo" (Podcast interview) - In this engaging podcast interview conducted by Kara Swisher, David Filo discusses his journey with Yahoo and shares valuable insights into the tech industry. Filo's candid responses provide a unique perspective on entrepreneurship, leadership, and the future of technology.

Online Resources

1. Yahoo.com - Explore the official website of Yahoo to learn more about its current offerings and services. Discover the latest news, finance, sports, and entertainment updates, and explore the history of Yahoo through its own lens.

2. "The History of Yahoo!" by WhoIsHostingThis? - This comprehensive online resource provides a detailed timeline of Yahoo's history, from its humble beginnings to its role as a global internet powerhouse. It also covers key milestones and acquisitions that shaped Yahoo's growth.

3. "David Filo" on Wikipedia - Visit David Filo's Wikipedia page for a concise overview of his life, work, and contributions to the tech industry. The page provides links to related topics, interviews, and external resources for further exploration.

Online Courses

1. "Introduction to Computer Science and Programming in Python" by MIT OpenCourseWare - This free online course, developed by MIT, provides an excellent introduction to computer science and programming fundamentals. By gaining a solid understanding of these concepts, you'll be equipped to better comprehend the technical aspects of David Filo's journey.

2. "Web Design for Everybody" by University of Michigan on Coursera - Explore the world of web design and development with this beginner-friendly

online course. By learning the basics of HTML, CSS, and JavaScript, you'll gain a deeper appreciation for the technical aspects of David Filo's accomplishments.

Podcasts

1. "Masters of Scale" with Reid Hoffman - Dive into the stories of legendary entrepreneurs and innovators with this popular podcast series hosted by Reid Hoffman, co-founder of LinkedIn. While not directly focused on David Filo or Yahoo, the series provides valuable insights on scaling businesses and navigating the ever-changing tech industry.

2. "Acquired" with Ben Gilbert and David Rosenthal - Join Ben Gilbert and David Rosenthal as they dissect the greatest technology acquisitions and IPOs of our time. Their engaging discussions provide unique perspectives on the challenges and triumphs faced by companies like Yahoo.

Tech News Websites

1. TechCrunch (`www.techcrunch.com`) - Stay up-to-date with the latest news and analysis of the tech industry, including startups, venture capital, and emerging technologies. TechCrunch offers a diverse range of content, providing valuable insights into the evolving landscape of the tech world.

2. Mashable (`www.mashable.com`) - Explore the intersection of technology, culture, and entertainment with Mashable. Discover engaging articles and thought-provoking features that explore the impact of technology on various aspects of our lives.

These resources should provide you with a wealth of information and perspectives to deepen your understanding of David Filo's journey, Yahoo's impact on the internet, and the broader tech industry. Happy exploring!

Index

A comprehensive index of names, places, and events mentioned in the book

Quick reference for specific topics or details

In this section, we provide a quick reference for specific topics and details related to the life and legacy of David Filo and the birth of Yahoo. This reference guide will assist the readers in easily finding specific information, navigating through the book, and enhancing their overall reading experience. It includes key names, places, events, and important concepts mentioned throughout the biography.

- **David Filo:** Co-creator of Yahoo, an internet entrepreneur, and a renowned computer programmer.
- **Jerry Yang:** Co-founder of Yahoo and David Filo's Stanford University roommate.
- **Yahoo:** The internet search engine and web directory founded by David Filo and Jerry Yang.
- **Stanford University:** The prestigious university where David Filo and Jerry Yang studied and developed the initial version of Yahoo.
- **Dot-com bubble:** A speculative bubble in the late 1990s and early 2000s, characterized by excessive investment in internet-based companies.
- **Google:** The search engine that emerged as a strong competitor to Yahoo in the early 2000s.
- **Verizon Communications:** The telecommunications company that acquired Yahoo in 2017.

- **Tech industry:** The industry that encompasses companies and individuals involved in the development and production of technological innovations.
- **Internet:** The global network of interconnected computers that enables the sharing of information and resources.
- **Web directory:** A website that provides categorization and indexing of web pages, allowing users to find relevant information.
- **Acquisitions:** The process of buying other companies or their assets to expand one's business.
- **Philanthropy:** The practice of giving and donating for the welfare of others, often involving charitable organizations or endeavors.
- **Legacy:** The lasting impact and influence of a person or organization on a particular field or industry.
- **Tech world:** The collective industry, community, and network of individuals involved in technology development and innovation.
- **Search engine:** A software system that retrieves data and information from a database in response to user queries.
- **Global internet powerhouse:** A company or organization that achieves significant influence and dominance in the internet industry on a global scale.
- **Departure from Yahoo:** David Filo's decision to step down or leave his active role in Yahoo's operations.
- **Tech industry:** A term used to describe the collective industry, community, and network of individuals involved in technology development and innovation.
- **Lessons learned:** Insights and wisdom gained from experiences and challenges faced in one's personal and professional life.
- **The future of technology and the internet:** Speculations, predictions, and possibilities regarding technological advancements and the evolution of the internet.

- **Yahoo's acquisition by Verizon Communications:** The transaction in which Verizon Communications purchased Yahoo, leading to significant changes and integration between the two companies.
- **The changing landscape of the internet:** The evolving environment, trends, and dynamics in the internet industry and user behavior.
- **Yahoo's place in history:** The historical significance and contributions of Yahoo to the development of the internet and the tech industry as a whole.
- **Timeline:** A chronological sequence of events and milestones in David Filo's life, as well as important moments in Yahoo's history.
- **Accomplishments and awards:** Recognitions, honors, and achievements received by David Filo and Yahoo over the years.
- **Other notable events:** Significant occurrences and developments related to David Filo, Yahoo, and the tech industry, apart from the major milestones.
- **Impact on the tech industry and internet:** The influence, effects, and consequences of David Filo's work and Yahoo's success on the broader technology and internet landscape.

This quick reference provides a snapshot of the essential terms and topics covered throughout the biography. For more detailed information, readers are encouraged to refer to the corresponding sections in the book and explore the comprehensive index for a thorough understanding of the life and legacy of David Filo, the birth of Yahoo, and the impact on the tech industry and internet as a whole.

Remember, knowledge is power, and the more we understand the history and contributions of remarkable individuals like David Filo and the organizations they create, the better equipped we are to shape the future of technology and innovation.

Now, let's dive into the fascinating journey of David Filo and Yahoo, and explore the profound impact they had on the tech industry and the internet.

Ensuring easy navigation for readers

In order to provide a seamless reading experience, this section will discuss the various strategies employed to ensure easy navigation for readers. Navigating through a book can be a daunting task, especially when searching for specific information or topics. To address this challenge, we have implemented several features and design principles to make the navigation process as smooth as possible.

Chapter and section structure

One of the fundamental aspects of this book's design is a well-structured chapter and section organization. Each chapter delves into a specific topic, while sections within chapters focus on different subtopics. This hierarchical structure allows readers to quickly identify the information they are looking for.

To make navigation easier, we have included clear headings and subheadings for each chapter and section. These headings are informative, concise, and highlight the main ideas discussed in that particular segment. Additionally, the table of contents provides an overview of the book's structure, allowing readers to locate specific chapters or sections at a glance.

Index

The comprehensive index at the end of the book serves as a valuable tool for readers to quickly find specific topics or details. The index contains references to names, places, and events mentioned throughout the book. We have meticulously curated the index to ensure accuracy and relevance. By referring to the index, readers can jump directly to the relevant pages instead of scrolling through the entire book.

Quick reference

To facilitate easy access to specific topics or details, we have included a quick reference section within the index. This section highlights key concepts, equations, or definitions mentioned in the book. Readers can refer to this section for a concise overview and jump to relevant pages for in-depth explanations.

Visual aids and diagrams

We believe that visual aids play a crucial role in enhancing the reader's understanding and navigation. Throughout the book, we have incorporated diagrams, graphs, and illustrations generated using TikZ. These visual aids serve as visual representations of complex ideas and help readers grasp concepts more quickly.

For example, when discussing the growth of Yahoo, we include a timeline graph showcasing key milestones in Yahoo's history. This graph enables readers to visualize the development of Yahoo and understand its impact on the internet industry.

Cross-referencing

To connect related information across different chapters and sections, we have implemented cross-referencing. When a concept or topic is mentioned in one section, we provide references to other relevant sections where readers can find additional information. This feature allows readers to explore related concepts without tedious searching.

For instance, when discussing the challenges faced by Yahoo during the dot-com bubble, we cross-reference to the section on Yahoo's strategy to weather the storm. This enables readers to navigate seamlessly between related topics and gain a comprehensive understanding.

Interactive exercises

In addition to the traditional text-based content, we have included interactive exercises to engage readers and reinforce their understanding of the material. These exercises encourage readers to apply the concepts they have learned and test their knowledge. We provide detailed solutions to the exercises, enabling readers to assess their performance and further deepen their understanding.

Online resources

To further enhance navigation and provide additional resources for exploration, we have compiled a list of online sources and research materials. This reference list serves as a gateway to further readings, research papers, and articles related to the topics discussed in the book. By including this list, we ensure that readers have access to a wealth of information beyond the scope of this book.

Tricks and tips

Throughout the book, we include practical tips and tricks related to programming, technology, and internet entrepreneurship. These nuggets of wisdom provide readers with insights and shortcuts gathered from experienced professionals in the field. By incorporating these unconventional yet relevant tips, we aim to enhance the readers' knowledge and hone their skills.

For example, in the section discussing Yahoo's attempts to catch up with Google's search dominance, we include a tip on optimizing search engine algorithms. This tip offers programmers a practical approach to improve search functionality in their own projects.

Real-world examples

To make the content more relatable and applicable, we have included real-world examples and case studies throughout the book. These examples shed light on how the concepts discussed in each chapter are applied in real-life scenarios. By drawing connections between theory and practice, readers can better relate to the content and understand its relevance.

For instance, when discussing the impact of Yahoo on the internet, we include a case study on how Yahoo's search engine revolutionized online information retrieval. This example provides readers with a tangible example of Yahoo's influence.

Overall, the combination of well-structured chapters, a comprehensive index, clear headings, helpful visual aids, cross-referencing, interactive exercises, online resources, practical tips, and real-world examples ensures that readers can navigate through this book with ease. By incorporating these features, we aim to create an engaging and accessible reading experience that enables readers to quickly find the information they need and make meaningful connections between the various topics discussed.

Accessible searching for specific information

In our fast-paced digital world, the ability to find specific information quickly and efficiently is crucial. In this section, we will explore some practical strategies for conducting accessible searches and locating specific information with ease.

Leveraging search engines

Search engines are our gateway to the vast amount of information available on the internet. To conduct an effective search, it's important to understand how search engines work and how to use them to our advantage.

Choosing the right search engine While Google may be the most well-known search engine, it's not the only one available. Depending on your specific information needs, you may find that other search engines can provide more tailored results. For example, if you're searching for academic research papers, you might consider using Google Scholar or other specialized academic search engines.

Using advanced search techniques To narrow down your search results and find specific information, you can use advanced search techniques. One common technique is to use quotation marks to search for an exact phrase. For example, searching for "David Filo" will only return results that include this exact phrase, rather than individual instances of the words "David" and "Filo" separately.

Additionally, you can use Boolean operators, such as "AND," "OR," and "NOT," to refine your search. For example, searching for "David Filo" AND "Yahoo" will only return results that include both the name "David Filo" and the word "Yahoo."

Exploring specialized databases

While search engines are great for finding general information, sometimes you may need to access specialized databases to find specific information in a particular field or industry. Here are a few examples:

Academic databases If you're conducting research for an academic paper or project, academic databases can be a valuable resource. Some popular academic databases include JSTOR, EBSCOhost, and PubMed. These databases contain a vast array of scholarly articles, research papers, and other academic resources.

Technical documentation For programmers and developers, accessing technical documentation can be crucial. Many software companies provide documentation libraries or knowledge bases that contain detailed information about their products, APIs, and programming languages. Utilizing these resources can help you find answers to specific coding questions or better understand the capabilities of a particular software tool.

Industry-specific databases In certain industries, there may be specialized databases that contain valuable information. For example, in the healthcare industry, there are databases like Medline or PubMed that focus on medical research and literature. Likewise, financial professionals can utilize databases like Bloomberg or Morningstar to access financial data and analysis.

Online forums and communities Sometimes the best source of specific information comes from real-world experiences or discussions with fellow experts. Online forums and communities, such as Stack Overflow for programming or Quora for general knowledge, can be great places to ask specific questions and get answers from knowledgeable individuals.

Improving search efficiency

Finding specific information quickly requires efficient searching techniques. Here are a few strategies to improve your search efficiency:

Using specific keywords When searching for specific information, it's important to use precise and relevant keywords. Think about the specific terms or phrases that are likely to be present in the information you're seeking. Using specific keywords will help you retrieve more accurate and targeted search results.

Refining search queries If your initial search query doesn't yield the desired results, don't give up. Instead, try refining your search query by adding more specific keywords or using advanced search techniques. Experimenting with different search queries can often lead to better results.

Utilizing search filters Most search engines provide filters or advanced search options. These filters allow you to narrow down your search results by criteria such as date, file type, language, or website domain. Utilizing these filters can help you quickly find the specific information you're looking for.

Bookmarking useful resources When you come across a valuable resource or website that provides specific information, consider bookmarking it for future reference. By creating a well-organized collection of bookmarks, you can easily access specific information without the need for repetitive searches.

Remember, searching for specific information requires a combination of effective strategies, critical thinking, and persistence. By leveraging search engines, exploring specialized databases, and implementing efficient searching techniques, you'll be well-equipped to find the specific information you need in a timely manner.

Resources

1. *How to Use Search Operators and Boolean Operators for Better Google Search*: An article by Moz.com that provides in-depth information on how to use search operators and Boolean operators effectively.

2. *10 Best Websites for Academic Research Papers*: A blog post by EdTechReview that highlights the top 10 websites for finding academic research papers and articles.

3. *Top 10 Programming Q&A Websites*: A list compiled by Hongkiat.com of the top 10 programming Q&A websites, where you can ask specific coding questions and get answers from experts.

Exercises

1. Identify a specific topic or question that you need to find information about. Use advanced search techniques, such as quotation marks and Boolean operators, to conduct a search and locate relevant information.

2. Explore a specialized database related to your field or industry (e.g., academic database, technical documentation, industry-specific database). Locate a specific piece of information that is relevant to your current work or interests.

3. Visit an online forum or community related to your expertise or interests (e.g., Stack Overflow, Quora). Ask a specific question and evaluate the quality of the responses you receive.

Note: The exercises are designed to improve your skills in accessing specific information efficiently. It is important to adapt the exercises based on your field or area of interest for optimal learning.

Enhancing the overall reading experience

In this section, we will explore ways to enhance the overall reading experience for our readers. A well-designed index is an important component of any book, and it can greatly improve the accessibility and usability of the content. We will discuss the importance of a comprehensive index, the benefits of quick reference, and the use of accessible searching to make information easily retrievable.

The Importance of a Comprehensive Index

A comprehensive index serves as a roadmap that allows readers to quickly navigate through the information presented in the book. It is an invaluable tool for finding specific topics or details without having to read the entire text. In the case of our biography of David Filo, a well-organized index will allow readers to easily locate information about key events in his life, his contributions to the tech industry, and the impact of Yahoo on the internet.

To create a comprehensive index, we need to identify the key names, places, and events mentioned in the book. It is important to include relevant subtopics and cross-references to ensure that readers can find related information easily. For example, under the entry for "Yahoo's first funding," we could include cross-references to the section on acquisitions and new ventures to provide readers with a broader understanding of the company's growth.

Benefits of Quick Reference

In addition to a comprehensive index, a quick reference section can further enhance the reading experience. This section would provide readers with concise summaries or bullet points of the main topics covered in the book. It acts as a condensed version of the content and allows readers to quickly refresh their memory or find specific information without going through the entire text.

For example, in our biography, the quick reference section could include a summary of David Filo's contributions to the tech industry, such as his role in the development of the web directory concept and the growth of Yahoo as a dominant internet brand. This section would serve as a handy reference for readers who want a quick overview of the key points covered in the book.

Accessible Searching for Specific Information

With the advancement of digital technology, readers increasingly expect instant access to information. Adding an accessible searching feature to the book can greatly improve the reading experience. This can be accomplished by providing a digital version of the book that allows readers to search for specific keywords or phrases.

By including an offline index or a search function within the digital version, readers will be able to quickly find the information they are looking for. They can search for specific names, places, or events mentioned in the book and jump directly to the relevant sections. This feature is particularly useful for readers who want to review specific topics or conduct in-depth research.

Additional Strategies

To further enhance the overall reading experience, we can incorporate visual elements such as diagrams, graphs, or illustrations. These visual aids can help readers better understand complex concepts or visualize historical events. For example, we could include a timeline of David Filo's life and career, highlighting key milestones and accomplishments.

To engage the readers and reinforce their learning, we can include exercises or reflection questions at the end of each chapter. These exercises can range from simple comprehension questions to more thought-provoking prompts that encourage readers to apply the lessons learned from David Filo's journey to their own lives.

Lastly, to make the reading experience more enjoyable, we can include anecdotes or personal stories to humanize the content. Sharing lesser-known facts or behind-the-scenes moments can create a connection between the readers and the subject of the biography.

Conclusion

In this section, we discussed various strategies to enhance the overall reading experience for our audience. By creating a comprehensive index, providing a quick reference section, and incorporating accessible searching, readers will be able to navigate through the content with ease. Additionally, visual aids, exercises, and personal anecdotes can further engage the readers and make the reading experience more enjoyable. By implementing these techniques, we can ensure that our biography of David Filo not only informs but also entertains and inspires future programmers.

Index

9 781779 699374

Printed by Libri Plureos GmbH in Hamburg,
Germany